gerry turcotte

big
things

ORDINARY
THOUGHTS IN
EXTRAORDINARY
TIMES

FOREWORD BY GARY STROTHER

NOVALIS

© 2019 Novalis Publishing Inc.

Cover design: Martin Gould
Cover image: Photawa/iStockphoto
Layout: Audrey Wells

Published by Novalis

Publishing Office
1 Eglinton Avenue East, Suite 800
Toronto, Ontario, Canada
M4P 3A1

Head Office
4475 Frontenac Street
Montréal, Québec, Canada
H2H 2S2

www.novalis.ca

Cataloguing in Publication is available from Library and Archives Canada.

ISBN: 978-2-89688-626-5

Printed in Canada.

We acknowledge the support of the Government of Canada.

5   4   3   2   23   22   21   20   19

contents

Weekly Reflections

dedication

Stories Count

You can never underestimate the power of a good story. It might be in the form of an anecdote, a reflection, a personal experience or even a joke. Now assemble a collection of thoughtful stories that were created through the lens of a master storyteller and you come up with *Big Things: Ordinary Thoughts in Extraordinary Times*.

I have been directly involved in education my entire life. First as a student, and then for over 35 years as a teacher, administrator, and presently as the Chief Superintendent of the largest Catholic school board in the province of Alberta. My wife was a highly decorated teacher, my eldest son is a wonderful new teacher in our district, and our youngest is well into his Education degree. Teaching and learning is in our blood and is often the topic of conversation around the Sunday dinner table. I have been so fortunate to witness expert teachers at many levels deliver complex theories and lessons by relating the concept to a simple story. A story that resonates, is contextual and brings a thought to life. Gerry Turcotte is one of those special teachers, and has been for many years.

Through Turcotte's previous work, *Small Things: Reflections on Faith and Hope*, I was introduced to the telling of short stories that not only entertained me, but also afforded me the opportunity to share them with our staff, expressing multifaceted ideas in an ingenious fashion. Stories that bring our faith to life and share the good news without being preachy or condescending. I have been fortunate enough to hear Gerry convey some of these stories in person, and he does that skillfully, but I was amazed at how beautifully they came across on paper.

As I was about to pick up this book for the first time, a friend of mine was flipping through the story titles. He remarked at how the topics seemed to make a nice connection between the past and present. Right off the bat in "The Air That We Breathe," we learn that a small part of the atmosphere is recirculated indefinitely. We are breathing in the same air of the conversations of Jesus and those present at the Last Supper. I then jumped to "Note to Selfie," where we read about the use of technology in the hands of vulnerable individuals whose judgment may not be as sophisticated as we hope. As a result, this can lead to the making of some very poor choices. I'd say those two examples epitomize the very nature of past to present!

The title "Hamster Sandwiches" immediately piqued my curiosity, and I was not disappointed. I laughed out loud when Turcotte relayed the story of a student who told him they were bilingual in three languages before submitting an essay that proved they were literate in none. "My Career as an Altar Boy" also left a smile on my face, as we are treated to a story of perhaps the only altar boy to ever be fired after his first shift. Not only is there humour to be found, but it also strikes a poignant note, as we are given a glimpse into Gerry's personal life and the unconditional support he received from his mother. These little snippets into the author's past give many of the stories real depth; you can't help but be connected to him.

Over the past several years, Gerry Turcotte has been the driving force behind the fastest-growing university in Alberta: St. Mary's University. Small classes, caring staff and a commitment to personal attention are hallmarks of this institution. I can personally attest to the quality of the graduates, as some of our district's most successful new teachers have honed their craft at St. Mary's. At the core of this school is a deep commitment to faith, social justice, academia and introducing keen minds to a well-rounded experience that will serve them well in their desired fields. St. Mary's also attracts special partners and champions, like Tom and Debra Mauro, to whom this book is dedicated. Folks like these make an impact simply by their involvement in a project, and if they are indeed involved, it can be assured it is for a good reason.

Throughout our lives, we have been treated to the amazing stories of Jesus in the parables. He was able to make the lesson behind each story understandable and thought provoking, allowing us to grow deeper in our faith. Our Indigenous brothers and sisters have long used stories to convey their history and lessons to help us learn in this same way.

Sykes Powderface, a Chiniki Band Elder, spoke to the oral nature of relaying the history of the Indigenous people. He asked, "Are you listening?" He went on to say, "If you have listened and have heard what is said, then you will act on it."

This beautiful collection of stories allows us to take some time to listen, to reflect and to grow. Hopefully, we'll pull meaning out of a few of these gems and act on them. That's how we can make these stories count...

Gary Strother, Chief Superintendent,
Calgary Catholic School District

From Little Things Big Things Grow

It is like a mustard seed, which, when sown upon the ground,
is the smallest of all the seeds on earth;
yet when it is sown it grows up and becomes
the greatest of all shrubs.

Mark 4:26-34

L ittle did I think that the occasional columns I began to write in 2011 would grow into a briefly syndicated column and generate two books. So it was, however, that "Figure of Speech," which started as a column for the Catholic monthly publication *The Carillon*, which was circulated to local parishes in the diocese of Calgary, Alberta, soon began to appear in *The Western Catholic Reporter, The Prairie Messenger* and now *The Catholic Register*, with occasional columns appearing in the *Calgary Herald, The Kolbi Times* and other publications. The columns, which began as celebrations of specific St. Mary's University initiatives, morphed into meditations on any and all matters related to the faith life writ large.

When Novalis published *Small Things: Reflections on Faith and Hope*, bringing together the best columns of the previous three years, I was certain that this was the culmination of the project, not its middle point. And yet the ideas kept flowing. *Big Things* is a response to this continued conversation. As with the first book, this is not a theological treatise. I am at pains to point out that I am not a theologian but a writer and commentator, and one who has brought his own eclectic way of looking at the world to the idea of faith in our times. Whether this is valid, appropriate or justifiable is for others to decide, but it remains true that I often explore my own faith through questions of grammar, odd photographs, and, God forbid, church notices.

As odd as this might be on one level, on another it makes perfect sense. Our faith life permeates everything we do. It should guide our decisions, but it's also true that it resides in everything, even when we're oblivious to its influence. And sometimes you need to tease this out and discover the Divine in the unexpected. *Big Things* makes no claim to big ideas. This is not a book that will redefine anyone's faith life, or answer burning questions that have been troubling theologians for centuries. It is, instead, a humble work, seeking to entertain through the celebration of faith and ideas. It is certainly not a mustard seed in any sense that the Gospel writers mean. But the parable is not entirely unrelated, either.

Through these columns I have met hundreds of people. I have, by virtue of the rather unfortunately aged photo that accompanies the columns, been recognized by parishioners as I've travelled throughout Alberta. I've received letters from readers in other provinces. And I have shared stories with people I had no hope of meeting. This is a gift of immeasurable, and entirely unanticipated, worth. Such is the way small things grow. And for this I am ever so thankful.

Despite the playful nature of my columns, I hope my serious commitment to social justice shines through. The title of this introduction isn't merely a pun on the titles of both books. As someone who lived in Australia for 25 years, I have long been haunted by Paul Kelly's powerful anthem to reconciliation and Indigenous rights. Kelly's song "From Little Things, Big Things Grow" celebrates the Aboriginal land rights and self-determination movements Down Under, and became a rallying cry for people of good heart throughout Australia.

But it became an anthem, of sorts, for any grassroots movement, where small Davids took on Goliaths, and it continues to resonate that way for me today. All social justice initiatives begin with a small voice that is amplified by conviction and belief. It is the story of community groups everywhere. And so it is, I hope, with faith. The small seed that is planted inside us should grow and burst out to influence the world. If it is true, as I discuss in the opening column, that parts of the air we breathe never evaporate, and recirculate indefinitely from time immemorial, then we must speak truth to power and raise our voices for those who can't, because what we breathe will live on forever. Literally!

All this makes my columns seem grander than they are, and I don't mean for it to come across that way. Whatever small interest these musings can generate will be good enough for me. I thank the many selfless people who have helped to make these columns better than they might otherwise have been. Thank you first and foremost to Dr. Helen Kominek, who always had first crack at these and whose honest feedback, and occasional evisceration, was never misplaced.

Thank you to Monique Achtman, editor of *The Carillon*, where many of these first appeared; and to Maureen Weber of *The Prairie Messenger* and Glen Argan of *The Western Catholic Reporter*, who gave these columns a home, provided insight into improving them, and always made me feel part of their publication teams. It was with a heavy heart that I learned that the two latter publications were being discontinued after decades of sterling service to the community, and that *The Carillon* was being scaled back. Hopefully, the work they did in celebrating our faith life will be championed and remembered.

Thank you to Bill and Laura Locke, editors of *The Kolbi Times*, for the columns they commissioned, and to Lindsay Gurevitch of *Reimagine Magazine* for publishing "The Biophilia Hypothesis" in celebration of the restoration of the university's nearly 100-year-old water tower. And thank you to Jim O'Leary, editor of *The Catholic Register*, for giving my columns a new home so the story can continue.

In the end, I can only hope that these columns resonate for many, amuse others, and perhaps even inspire new ways to approach our faith life for some. That would be no small thing.

Gerry Turcotte

The Air That We Breathe

*In his hand is the life of every living thing
and the breath of every human being.*

Job 12:10

Famed astronomer the late Harlow Shapley once ruminated on a remarkable notion. He explained that some components of our air, and especially the argon atoms that comprise 1% of our atmosphere, recirculate indefinitely. Unlike ozone gases, these components of the air that we breathe never really disappear. They pass through the body virtually untouched and then re-enter the atmosphere. As Shapley put it, "Your next breath will contain more than 400,000 of the argon atoms that Gandhi breathed in his long life. Argon atoms are here from the conversations at the Last Supper, from the arguments of diplomats at Yalta, and from the recitations of the classic poets."

We think of ourselves as removed from the distant past, and perhaps only tangentially connected to Jesus. So this theory is especially wonderful because it reminds us that we carry within us the breath of those who sat at the Last Supper. That we are not only symbolically a part of that ancient event, but also actually participants at the table of our Lord. It changes how we might think of Holy Communion, reminding us of a shared and sacred feast, not just of bread and wine … but breath!

I remember once discussing historical events with one of my classes, and a somewhat jaded student saying, "What does it matter? It's all ancient history and it has nothing to do with us!" I forget what class it was, but I will never forget the question. It's relevant and legitimate, even if it is misinformed. The reality is that we are all connected, always and everywhere. We always implore leaders to learn from the mistakes of the past and not repeat them. The reality, however, is that we seem unable to learn. We continue to repeat the same injuries, trigger new wars, and turn our backs on our fellow human beings. Is it possible that we do this because we fail to understand how deeply we are all connected, and how an injury to one is an injury to all?

Shapley's theory puts all this into remarkable perspective. We are breathing air that passed through the lungs of dinosaurs and prehistoric beings; Antony and Cleopatra; Shakespeare; and yes, we are breathing the words of Jesus. We exhale them into the lives and spirit of our children. We share a breath that all of our brothers and sisters the world over have had a part in shaping. It's a sobering thought that reminds us we are not alone, and we bear the responsibility to remain connected to our neighbours near and far. Frankly, the thought of it takes my breath away.

A Higher Craft

He gives to all of them their names.

Psalm 147:4

I grew up in a hardware store. Not the fancy big box stores that occupy acres of inner-city landscapes. My dad's store was a small, rundown shack that he built as far out in the city as he could in order to afford the land. And then, year after year, we would surreptitiously build small extensions to the structure when we knew the city inspectors weren't working. And so the little building grew inexorably and at times grotesquely. I once came back from summer camp to discover the front door to our house had been moved. "I needed more storage space," my dad explained matter-of-factly. "Where's the door?" I asked. He pointed to a gloomy hole under the stairwell. It looked appalling. "Mom won't like that," I muttered. Dad nodded. "Yeah, she's staying at her sister's for a few days."

One year, worn down by the hours he spent in the poorly heated store, my father decided to cut a hole in the living room floor of the apartment he had built above the shop. His plan was to install a trap door in the floor and hang an electric buzzer nearby that was connected to the front entrance so that whenever a customer came in, he'd know. The idea was that he could sit in the heated upstairs, get his paperwork done, and then climb down whenever someone needed to be served. The flaw in the plan was that he would have to cut through my mother's recently purchased plush carpeting, the first new thing he'd bought her in years. "I really don't think this will go down well," I started to say, but my father shook his head. "You have to be positive about change, son. Don't be a defeatist." He paused, deep in thought. "We'll wait until she goes away for the weekend."

While heartbreaking for my mom, the changing space was a joy for a young boy. There were crawl spaces that materialized out of thin air, trap doors leading to nowhere, and false walls that were the envy of any medieval castle—except for the fact that they were made out of discarded plaster instead of 1,000-year-old granite. And the hardware, too, was magical. There were tools for every task, screws and eyelets for every purpose, and an infinite variety of odds and sods for every plumbing task under the sun. For a kid who read the dictionary for fun, reading the catalogue of hardware goods was even cooler. "What are these?" I'd ask my dad, lost in the contents of a brick-thick order book. "Aglets," he'd say, "to hold the tips of shoelaces together." He said it as though he were describing the most ordinary thing in the world. In reality he was naming the magic of the universe, as it lived in the objects of the everyday.

Is it too much to believe that God, in his infinite wisdom, lived in all of these quirks and quarks? At Mass I tried desperately to memorize the objects of the church—the chasuble, the ambo, the mitre or the monstrance—and felt somehow that there was an infinite divine in the names of all things. Yes, it spoke of human creativity, but surely it also provided evidence of a higher craft—a creativity that far outshone the reaches of our own imaginings. I don't think my mother always saw it that way, but when she spoke of love, especially for my dad in spite of his infuriating schemes, you could almost sense her understanding of a deeper mystery. I'm sure there's a name for that as well.

Singing a Different Tune

I will solve my riddle to the music of the harp.

Psalm 49:4

S everal years ago, when my daughter decided she wanted to learn to play the piano, a good friend tracked down a used upright for us on Kijiji. Even though it was on its last legs, Sophie was able to spend almost two years learning the basic skills until a better instrument was needed. When we discovered that the soundboard on the first piano was irreparably damaged, it became a large, useless, dust-collecting sculpture in the dining room. Recently, another friend sent me a website featuring creative ideas to repurpose otherwise dead pianos. One of these caught my fancy, so on New Year's Eve, my son and I began dismantling the upright and slowly converting it into a writing desk, built on the exposed skeleton of the once noble instrument. It will live again!

The timing of this project is relevant. I always follow a number of rituals on New Year's Day. One of these is to engage in key priority activities, on the unscientific premise that how you start your year will be a template for how the rest of it unfolds. For me this means spending quality time with my family, completing one important work task and starting a creative project. I also set aside time for meditation and prayer. This, inevitably, compels me to review issues that matter, priorities for the year ahead, fears and successes, goals and objectives. And it is always a time to say thank you for the blessings in my life, no matter how difficult the prior year has been.

I don't want to draw an overly long bow here, but it seems to me that the repurposed piano is a more useful metaphor for the new year than the cliché of starting from scratch. The reality is that we begin each year by repurposing the last. We may acknowledge things that are no longer working for us and try to change them, but we inevitably build on the foundation of the past. The start of the calendar year should offer an opportunity to expose our core, figure out how we're put together, acknowledge the beauty of who we are and how God made us, and reimagine the possibilities for transformation. Like our humble piano, we should be true to who we are, even while playing a different tune. The important thing is to always look for the potential within every object, situation and individual, and then find ways to help that potential emerge. That's an upright resolution if ever there was one.

Play It Again, Stan!

I have seen a limit to all perfection.

Psalm 119:96

My mother always misremembered sayings. "Better late than lost," she might say, or "Early to bed, and you get up even earlier." It was charming, and I thought of her often when I encountered characters in literature prone to misquotations. Catherine, the maid in Jules Verne's *Extraordinary Voyage*, is one of these. "He who laughs last, laughs from his backside," she announced, instead of "He who laughs last laughs best."

Sometimes misremembered sayings take on a life of their own. I was amazed to learn that the original lyrics to "The Twelve Days of Christmas" included the words "four colly birds" ("colly" meaning "black"). Over time, the misremembered phrase, rendered as "four calling birds," became the accepted norm. And who doesn't remember Bogart's famous line in *Casablanca* as "Play it again, Sam"? Well, he never actually said it—the phrase came from Woody Allen—but no one cares. (For the record, it's Ingrid Bergman's character, Ilsa Lund, who says, "Play it, Sam. Play," about the song "As Time Goes By.")

For me, though, the phenomenon of misremembering traces its way through my church memory. I have spoken before of my confusion over the "miserable chord" the priest kept referring to (instead of "Misericord"). And my mom, despite her own mistakes, was furious one year when I belted out, "Joy to the world, the Lord has gum!" during the Christmas carols. Later I took comfort in discovering that this was a shared misunderstanding. Malachy McCourt uses a misheard phrase from the Hail Mary as the title of his charming novel *A Monk Swimming*. As in "Hail Mary, full of grace, blessed art thou a monk swimming." This, as they say, is a perfect mondegreen, a word coined by American writer Sylvia Wright to mean a misremembered phrase.

Perhaps more fascinating is how we have participated in a rewriting of the Bible without realizing it, so that many sentences are spoken as gospel truth when in fact they don't appear in the holy book. The examples are many and surprising: "Spare the rod, spoil the child." "God works in mysterious ways." "The lion shall lie down with the lamb." "Cleanliness is next to Godliness." There are certainly passages that approximate the sentiment of many of these now established sayings, but that's about it.

I guess the takeaway message is simply this: we are flawed and imperfect, searching always for the *mot juste*, but finding only snippets of understanding. In some ways, this is reassuring. As Salvador Dali once put it, "Have no fear of perfection—you'll never reach it." Or as my mom might say: "Practice makes … a person very tired." Wise words to welcome in the new year!

A Noble Man

Whoever aspires to the office of bishop desires a noble task.

1 Timothy 3:1

While driving to work on January 4, 2016, I heard on the radio that the Bishop of the Diocese of Calgary, Fred Henry, was officially announcing his retirement after 19 years as bishop. While I had an inkling that this was coming, it was still a great shock to hear the news confirmed. As Chancellor of St. Mary's University, I had worked closely with him for five and a half years. This activity included convocations, opening and closing term liturgies on campus, and blessings at numerous events, including five Bishop's Dinners. I even recall, with some trepidation, a lone phone call very early in my presidency, where Bishop Henry asked me to join his foursome at a charity golf tournament. When the Bishop calls, you say yes. So I did. After hanging up I announced to my kids, "I have to learn how to play golf!" They weren't hopeful, and with good reason.

That tournament was one of the most stressful public events I have ever attended. To suggest that my game was execrable is to be charitable, and not in a fundraising way. In fact, as I moved towards the cart for the first time on that fateful day, someone leaned towards me. "He got two holes-in-one last year," the man whispered, no doubt trying to inspire confidence. "You know, Bishop," I said as we approached the first hole, "you'll need to be a bit patient. This is the first time I've ever golfed." Bishop Henry stared at me with those piercing eyes that would drive a lesser man to repent for sins undone: "Charity is for church," he declared. "This is golf. You're on your own." And as he prepared to tee off he added, "You know, I got two holes-in-one last year…." It should be said that Bishop Henry often mentioned my golf game and St. Jude in the same breath. I never knew why….

In interviews about Bishop Henry, I have been asked what people will most remember about his time in office. The gist of my answer is that we will remember a man of principle, conviction and energy; a man of faith and goodwill; a man unafraid to speak his mind and defend the mission of the Church, who spoke up for the voiceless, advocated for the homeless, and believed passionately in the importance of education. He is a man who inspires confidence and conviction—a brilliant raconteur who is welcoming in his humour and insight and who is never afraid to stand his ground.

But this is not a eulogy. Bishop Henry will remain a dynamic voice for the Catholic Church, the underdog and those who need his activism. In this sense I know that he will not go quietly into that good night. He will continue to champion our causes, and to generously offer his prayers and support … except, possibly, on the golf course. There, you're on your own!

A Knight's Tale

Serve one another with whatever gift each of you has received.
1 Peter 4:10

Both my father and my uncle were Knights of Columbus. Unfortunately, they were also inveterate pranksters, so when I asked them about becoming a Knight the picture they painted of the process almost drove me into therapy.

"The Knights?" my uncle said, raising his voice alarmingly, and then he melodramatically scanned the surroundings for spies and agitators. "You mean, *the* ... Knights?" He looked at my father, who inexplicably began to shake his head and mop his brow. Then began what can only be construed as a secret handshake performed by two men being electrocuted.

"I could tell you about them," my dad finally whispered, "but then I'd have to kill you." My uncle was quick to clarify: "Actually, even if we don't tell you, we may have to kill you. Just in case they're listening." "Who's listening?" I asked naively. "Can't tell you," said my dad. "But the initiation was hell. That's even more top secret."

They then went on to speak of their initiation ceremony, where they were made to scale enormous cliffs, live in an isolation chamber, eat raw goat (I think they suggested it was dead at the time, but my memory is a bit hazy on this), and then walk a high wire across sacred sites. It was at about that point that I began to understand that maybe I would never learn the truth until I myself became a Knight, but I still made a mental note to delay this as long as possible, just in case. I've never been a fan of goat.

I think it's safe to say that many people have a sense of curiosity about the Knights. Despite their incredible presence in the community, their extensive support of a staggering number of charities and social causes, the Knights are also rather humble players, supporting but rarely taking centre stage. Perhaps this is why they are so valued and respected.

St. Mary's University is the beneficiary of their legendary fundraising ability, and can proudly thank the Knights for the restoration of the building in which our Education program is housed: Fr. Michael J. McGivney Hall. Over 130 years after they were founded, the Knights continue to be a force for good in an age of need, and for this I will always be grateful to them.

And, for the record, I did not need to eat raw goat!

A Heroic Heart

Do you not know that the saints will judge the world?

1 Corinthians 6:2

Several years ago, I had the pleasure of attending a workshop for university presidents at Harvard. As part of that program we were given a tour of the campus. We listened as the guide raved about the institution's oldest surviving building, built between 1718 and 1720. Unbeknownst to the guide, one of our fellow presidents was from Ireland; he observed pragmatically that buildings on his campus dated to the 1590s! Such things, as we know, are relative. By coincidence, the group reconvened in Ireland some years later, and I recall discussing Down Cathedral, an Irish church built on the site of a Benedictine monastery that dates back to 1183. Down Cathedral is said to be the resting place of St. Patrick.

Stephen Gwynn once noted that the "list of Irish saints is past counting; but in it all no other figure is so human, friendly, and lovable as St. Patrick—who was an Irishman only by adoption." Like many of the saints in the Catholic canon, St. Patrick lived a life of adventure and heroism. He was captured by pirates as a teenager and made a slave; he travelled the high seas and then found a life of prayer and contemplation. He was a cleric, a bishop and eventually a saint. As a child, I knew him as the man who chased the snakes from Ireland (no doubt apocryphal), but came to know him more as the organizational pretext for some of the best music, Guinness and celebration I've ever experienced for any cultural holiday. March 17th is, I'm sure, a favourite for many, Irish or otherwise.

The reality is that wherever you go, the Irish have stamped their influence on host cultures. Their indelible literature, their heart-rending ballads, their irrepressible and subversive humour: the Irish are known for all of this and more. And St. Patrick's Day is both a legitimate reason and an unabashed pretext to celebrate all that is remarkable about the Irish. Indeed, the passion for Ireland is often as intense abroad as it is in the Emerald Isle itself. When I first moved to Australia many decades ago, I was adopted by a dedicated group of Irish expats who took me in as their own and immersed me so thoroughly in their sub-culture that I wondered if I'd travelled to Ireland by mistake.

Some years back, St. Mary's University hosted an Irish fundraising dinner. I remember discovering not only an inordinate number of staff and faculty suddenly claiming Irish ancestry, but also a surprising number of our students who had a passion for solo step dancing. The event was raucous, big-hearted and full of good cheer. In the moment, we were all Irish to the core. This, I think, is the gift of the Irish, and their gift to the world: for all the melancholy of their brilliant songs and stories, there's a heroic heart that beats mightily and welcomes all in the name of hope. Or as Pope John Paul II once said, "Love is never defeated." I could add, "The history of Ireland proves it." Happy St. Patrick's Day!

The Art of the Possible

Learn to do good; seek justice.

Isaiah 1:17

In July 2016 Pope Francis declared, "I want to be a spokesperson for the deepest longings of indigenous peoples. And I want you to add your voice to mine." In the video announcing his prayer intention, an Indigenous woman is shown approaching a podium and pleading for the plight of Indigenous peoples to be heard. When the camera pans out, however, the auditorium is empty: a metaphor, perhaps, for the deafness of the world to the plight of oppressed people.

It reminded me of a similar moment many years ago in Australia at a conference on listening to the Aboriginal voice. A young Indigenous scholar appeared before a large crowd of sympathetic white academics and played a video of an activist reading protest poetry. The sound was muted and the video was allowed to play, silently, for a full 15 minutes. All the while the presenter stared at the increasingly uncomfortable crowd. Then he turned off the TV and announced, before he stormed from the room, "This is what you've heard from Indigenous peoples at this conference." Horrified organizers realized, in that moment, that no Aboriginal guests had been invited to discuss the issue of Indigenous voices. It was a blunder that was not soon repeated.

I use the latter example because it occurred in the context of incredibly well meaning, learned and completely supportive academics at a conference specifically called to address acknowledged silence. Despite this, they still neglected to invite the people at the heart of the concern. It is a lesson I have never forgotten: that the greatest antidote to silence is dialogue, not speeches—action, not intentions. Even the most well-meaning person will be deaf to change unless we learn to listen.

In the context of the United Nations Declaration on the Rights of Indigenous Peoples, the recommendations of Canada's Truth and Reconciliation Commission, the inquiry into murdered and missing Aboriginal women and girls, and the recent controversy over the Canadian Catholic Church's handling of reparations owed over the handling of the residential schools debacle and the Pope's decision not to offer an official apology to Canada's Indigenous people, it seems more important than ever that conversations increase, not decrease.

For St. Mary's University in Calgary, this meant developing an Aboriginal Strategic Plan, which led to the establishment of an Elders on Campus program, an Indigenous Advisory Board, an experiential learning program at Ghost River for staff, faculty and students, and the incorporation of a blanket exercise modelling the devastating impact of colonialism held at a university retreat where 98% of the institution participated.

Of course, there is still much to do. What is heartening, however, is how fully the university as a whole has embraced this dialogue, and more importantly, how wonderfully Indigenous communities have welcomed St. Mary's into the dialogue: sharing their knowledge, their talents and their generosity of spirit.

Dialogue together with action is the first step towards reconciliation and healing. Our hope is that this journey towards reconciliation becomes widespread and all pervasive.

As Perry Bellegarde, national chief of the Assembly of First Nations, recently said, "Make room in your heart, your soul and your spirit." Or as Pope Francis put it at a ceremony in Chiapas, Mexico: "How worthwhile it would be for each of us to examine our conscience and learn to say, 'Forgive me!'"

Entertaining Angels

Do not neglect to show hospitality to strangers,
for by doing that some have entertained angels
without knowing it.

Hebrews 13:2

Recently I read a fascinating report that pointed out how driverless cars have accumulated more than twice the number of accidents as vehicles with drivers. But here's the interesting statistic: in 100% of those cases, the driverless car was not at fault. The reason for the higher accident rate? These cars always follow the rules. Now, it doesn't take a philosopher to analyze the interesting ethical conundrum this provides (though it would help). The dilemma facing programmers is how to make the cars safer if the only way of doing so is factoring in lawlessness. You can imagine the discussion during a board meeting at, say, Volkswagen: "Do we put a regulator on the car that will allow it to exceed the speed limit when merging, even if it breaks the law?" Of course they'd say no!

One of the other difficult questions engineers and programmers have asked is what they should do if a car is in danger of running over a child. Is it ethically acceptable to program the car, in this situation, to swerve off a cliff and sacrifice the passenger of the driverless vehicle? I wouldn't want to be the person making that decision, and certainly not by building in a universal program.

In reality, all of us make complex ethical decisions through-out our lives, some with more at stake than others. We also always analyze the rules to see how binding they are, because not every rule has the same value in different contexts. How many of us have told our children not to lie, but then urged them not to blurt out how much they hate grandma's cooking? Or what about the answer to "Does this make me look fat?" Context matters.

I thought of all this recently when reading an interview with Pope Francis. Once again, the pontiff reiterates the value of flex-ibility when interpreting God's laws. He stresses the importance of mercy and inclusion, even to the point of overlooking obscure teachings, urging us to "be surprised by reality, by a greater love or a higher standard." Jesus broke the law of Moses and reached out to the lepers, who were forbidden to have human contact. Not surprisingly, the Pope asks us to follow Jesus and to extend our hospitality to the margins. "Jesus goes and heals and inte-grates the marginalized, the ones who are outside the city, the ones outside the encampment. In so doing, he shows us the way." Sometimes the way is not only difficult to find, but also difficult to navigate. Only God's grace and an open, merciful heart can help us to follow the path Jesus would choose.

A New Commandment

"I give you a new commandment."
John 13:34

One of my favourite words is "Maundy." Growing up, I didn't know what Maundy Thursday meant. I just knew that it was a pretty serious time before Easter. For a while I used the word interchangeably with maudlin, and came to think of the maundies as relating to sadness and gloom. So it was with some surprise that I eventually learned it meant "commandment," from the Old French *mandé* and from the Latin *mandatum*. Its connection to church practice comes from Christ's own words: "*Mandātum novum dō vōbīs*," or "I give you a new commandment."

We celebrate Maundy Thursday in Holy Week, during the Mass of the Lord's Supper. It was there that Jesus washed the feet of his disciples. You will remember the dramatic retelling of this episode in John 13, when Jesus not only identifies Judas as his betrayer, but also humbles himself to wash the feet of his disciples. Peter appears to bristle at the intent, but Jesus explains: "Unless I wash you, you have no share with me." The point of the gesture, and one that Jesus insists on, is that this is a moment of communion with the other that must be passed on through all our relationships. "I have set you an example, that you also should do as I have done to you."

The obvious contemporary parallel to this behaviour has been modelled by Pope Francis, who time and again has chosen to wash the feet of the other: first youth at a detention centre, then prisoners and then women. More than his decision to live outside the papal palace or to eschew luxury vehicles, the Pope's washing of the feet is a deeply symbolic connection to Christ's demonstrated ministry. It is also an example of servant leadership, where the most humbling act brings the highest and lowest to the place of common bond where God first placed us.

It is perhaps because of this that Maundy Thursday matters so much, but also that we need to move past the bristling that Peter showed, especially when we look at those who are not like us: the outsider, the marginal, the struggling and the lost. Our need to look beyond formal rules and regulations and reach out, despite whatever fear or strangeness separates us, is not only important, but mandated. Christ did not come to make us comfortable; he came to make us grow. Are we prepared to turn away?

Lost & Found

"Celebrate and rejoice ... he was lost and has been found."
Luke 15:32

I t's hard to imagine getting through our daily lives without symbols. Few in the Western world would fail to recognize that a bright red octagon meant "Stop!" That is perhaps why there are so many funny additions to the sign. My favourites include the prankster who wrote "in the name of love" on one, or the person in a country town who crossed out "STOP" and wrote, "Whoa!" Not all symbols are as universally understood, however, and many have lost or changed their meaning over time.

Every Sunday at 4:30 p.m., St. Mary's University celebrates Mass, with our own priest and professor of psychology, Dr. Peter Doherty, presiding. This is a small gathering, though at times it has numbered up to 50 people, with the typical attendance around 20 or so. One particularly important part of the liturgy, made possible by the size of the group, is that the floor is opened after the homily for comments, questions and feedback from the assembly. At times the conversation is limited, with occasional bursts of insight breaking through the shyness; at other times the floodgates are opened and everyone, it seems, has something to contribute.

Recently it was a discussion of "The Prodigal Son," certainly one of the best-known parables in the Bible, and one that is deceptively straightforward. Perhaps what makes it most memorable for many is the dilemma faced by the loyal older brother when his profligate younger brother returns and is so enthusiastically embraced by their father. For our group discussion, much was made of the inevitability of the father's response, but also of the maligned older brother. Many of us, including me, noted the incredibly understandable, yet admittedly flawed, *humanness* of the older brother's bitterness. "For all these years I have been working like a slave for you, and I have never disobeyed your command; yet you have never given me even a young goat so that I might celebrate with my friends," he tells his father (15:29).

If "The Prodigal Son" continues to have such resonance 2,000 years after it was recorded, that is surely because it taps into our most human of failings. Yes, the older brother should understand the father's sheer joy at finding his lost son; but so, too, can we sympathize with the older one's confusion when he has been so faithful to his duties. One person at Mass that day also pointed out that the younger son returns not through conversion as such, but because he has become so destitute that he recognizes he would be better off even as a servant in his father's house. The father, however, welcomes his son with open arms.

What struck me afterwards was that the true power of the story—which is of course a metaphor for God's unconditional love—is that the actual moment of conversion does not occur when the youngest son crawls back to ask forgiveness, but in the extraordinarily comprehensive, love-filled forgiveness he receives. This is the power of God's embrace. When we witness the full-hearted acceptance, the joy of the Father's welcome, knowing how unworthy we are, it is impossible not to be moved and grateful beyond words. That, I suspect, is what even the older brother comes to realize … in his own good time.

The Flame of Compassion

How great a forest is set ablaze by a small fire!
James 3:5

T he fires of Fort McMurray in 2016 seemed to catalyze the world, proving once again how large the hearts of Albertans were at all times, but especially in moments of crisis. In the immediate aftermath of the fires, commentators speculated on what could have been done better and on how to prevent future such catastrophes. They inevitably drew comparisons to other fires: the Great Fire of London in 1666, where 70,000 of the city's 80,000 residents were left homeless; or the 2011 Great Slave Lake Fire in Alberta, where the entire community of 7,000 residents was evacuated. Many look to ongoing fires in California and British Columbia for additional reference points. In the end, however, what has been most remembered from that time are the tales of courage and compassion, celebrating the many who fought the fire, fled the inferno, assisted in housing the displaced, or raised money and collected supplies to help.

We remember the educators, like the principal at Father Turcotte School, who loaded a bus full of stranded students and fled the inferno, all the while staying in touch with anxious parents and guardians. We remember the fire chief who headed a campaign against "the Beast," leading a team of gallant and exhausted firefighters, many of whom had themselves lost their homes. We also remember the politician who called for unity rather than partisan politics, even as his home burned, and who only a year afterwards lost his son.

Seneca the Younger, one of early Rome's most famous philosophers, said that "Fire tests gold; suffering tests brave men"; his words are proven true in the aftermath of this tragedy. Possessions are lost, but courage prevails. The scale of the tragedy was enormous, but the relief effort was bigger. The churches were filled with prayer and compassion; the volunteers opened their hearts and gave of their time. Many post-secondary institutions opened their residences to the displaced. And charity was plentiful and moving: the eight-year-old girl who donated $100 of her own money; the runner who undertook a charity marathon even though he had never heard of Fort McMurray until the fire; the Syrian refugees who raised almost $4,000 for fire relief even though they themselves had recently lost everything they owned.

It is always difficult to put tragedies into context. At St. Mary's University, I looked at a photo of a staff member's street in Fort McMurray. Five houses with For Sale signs stood untouched by fire; hers, not for sale, was aflame. Who can say why bad things happen to good people? What is clear is that how we respond to tragedy is what defines the human spirit, and is what helps a community to heal. In that sense it's true to say that Fort McMurray will be stronger when it is rebuilt—not just because new infrastructure will be developed, but because every resident will know that the hearts of many are behind the reconstruction. This is the flame of compassion that is rebuilding the town.

A Hunting We Will Pokémon Go!

"Who is the man over there, walking in the field to meet us?"
Genesis 24:65

St. Mary's University in Calgary is apparently a hotspot for Pokémon GO! At all hours of the day or night, our campus is filled with people of all ages, moving between our library and classroom buildings through to our historic cairn, controversially unveiled by an allegedly inebriated Bing Crosby. I first heard of the phenomenon when my head of security called to alert me to potential dangers. He had just stopped someone who was driving his SUV in reverse across our lawns while looking at the screen of his phone. When he was pulled over, the man insisted he wasn't driving irresponsibly. He was merely "Looking for Pokémon," as though that explained it all.

We had one man leave his car in the middle of the main exit lane from the university, motor running, door open, with two infants strapped in the backseat while he hunted 10 metres away! A woman dragged one of our concrete dividers through the parking lot, unaware, apparently, that it was stuck beneath her car. The most remarkable moment that I witnessed was a young boy cycling within a metre of one of the many wild deer we have on campus, totally oblivious to the magnificent animal while fixated on an imaginary creature on his phone. Even the deer looked at him in amazement, though perhaps I'm projecting.

Despite the disruption, I have asked our facilities teams, indeed everyone on campus, to welcome these visitors. My son, who attends St. Mary's, sent me a photo of all his friends on campus one evening, surrounded by a dozen other people, all hunting Pokémon. I have walked beside a father and son as the latter patiently explained to his dad how to capture an elusive Kabutops. More than ever, there is a diversity of people on campus, strolling about, capturing mythical creatures and coming to know our campus, even indirectly, in a way that would not otherwise be possible.

This, too, is a manifestation of community; a university campus, like a classroom, has to welcome everyone. We are only as vital as the energy that walks across our grounds, and in this sense the Pokémon phenomenon has added to the diversity of our visitors. It's true that, as a Luddite, I wish they would put their phones away and look upon the marvel of this 35-acre site, cradled beside the largest urban provincial park in Alberta. On the other hand, it's good to see them here, being *with* nature if not exactly *of* it. And who knows, someone might accidentally stumble into our library and pick up a book. Stranger things have happened.

Easter Seals

"The hour has come for the Son of Man to be glorified."
John 12:23

As a child, I tended to take many things literally. I am surely not the only child who thought it grotesque to tell an actor to break a leg before they went on stage, or to be deeply confused when someone informed me their relative had kicked the bucket or bought the farm. So when Easter Seals first caught my attention in 1967, I can tell you I was mightily disappointed that no semi-aquatic mammals were part of that funding campaign for kids with disabilities. It was, however, one of the charities that always reminded me of Easter.

I think it's equally true to say that as a child, Easter similarly challenged me. First, the church was transformed for this day, not just by the unveiling of statues that had stood beneath rich purple coverings, but also because tons of people that I never saw at Mass suddenly showed up. This told me that something monumental was taking place, and that I should look at this event as particularly important. But I didn't quite get it.

As I grew older, however, I began to understand humility in a way that is profoundly connected to the life and death of Jesus, and that transforms this story of salvation into a language that made a great deal of sense to me as a human being encountering the world. It is now a comic cliché to point out how the word "literally" is misused: "I could literally eat a horse!" Really? But here is a moment in history where an act of leadership and sacrifice literally transforms our understanding of love.

The gift of Jesus is not only his teaching, but also his ultimate sacrifice. In his day, the thought of a messiah humbling himself to the point of persecution and humiliation was incomprehensible to many. But it is precisely this reversal of the paradigm of power that makes God's gift so overwhelming. And it becomes an example to all of us to put charity ahead of personal interests for the sake of true salvation. Easter is the moment when the world remembers this ultimate rebirth. That, surely, is something we can literally take to heart.

A Little Pencil in the Hand of a Writing God

Contribute to the needs of the saints;
extend hospitality to strangers.

Romans 12:13

In one of his most popular moves, Pope Francis canonized arguably the world's best-known contemporary religious figure: Mother Teresa, the "Saint of the Gutters." Born in Macedonia in 1910, Agnes Bojaxhiu would come to symbolize hope for the masses, making Calcutta and the Missionaries of Charity synonymous with selfless love. Catering to the poor and forgotten, the sick and the dying, she embraced people with HIV/AIDS, prostitutes and orphans equally, reminding us what constitutes true charity.

When she died on September 5, 1997, she left a hole in the world that will never be filled. Ironically, for all of the love and compassion we associate with Mother Teresa, those who knew her rarely describe her as a warm and fuzzy person. Everyone fortunate enough to meet her describes a passionate but ferocious individual, one who had little time for bureaucracy, niceties or diplomacy. She could dress down a bureaucrat, business tycoon or US president without hesitation. A friend of mine once told of a meeting where the world's top CEOs pulled out their chequebooks after one of her presentations. "I don't want your money," she informed them sternly. "I want you to go back to your community and make a difference." And so they did.

At St. Mary's University, our retired Professor of Religious Studies and Theology and CWL Chair for Catholic Studies, Dr. Michael Duggan, had the opportunity to meet Mother Teresa and, on one occasion, even have an extended conversation with her. While doing his doctoral studies at the Catholic University of America in Washington, DC, he taught classes to Mother Teresa's sisters at Gift of Peace, their home for the friends of Jesus who were elderly and homeless. That conversation is no doubt one of the reasons that Dr. Duggan remained so passionate about social justice issues at St. Mary's.

In his wonderful book *The Idea of Canada: Letters to a Nation*, former Governor General David Johnston praises the passion and influence of Mother Teresa—especially her ability to encourage charity. Certainly her gift for generating financial support for her missions is legendary, but so too is her message of hope and love for the unwanted and forgotten. It is here that we see the true focus of her passion and commitment. As Johnston puts it, she reminds us that every effort we make, no matter how small, "can reshape someone's life, if not the world."

Mother Teresa insisted that we should find joy in giving. And she reminded us that even the least among us—indeed *especially* the most unfortunate—"is Jesus in disguise." Perhaps my favourite quote from this new saint is this one: "I'm a little pencil in the hand of a writing God, who is sending a love letter to the world." No return address needed!

Breaking News

Peace be to the whole community.

Ephesians 6:23

It is difficult to ignore the news these days. Every report seems grim, from wars to economic turmoil to scandals. Everywhere we turn we see evidence of humanity's intolerance, greed and corruption. Watching the news recently, I simply had to change the channel. It's not so much that I want to bury my head in the sand, but at times the unrelenting negativity does wear me down.

What perked me up, I must confess, was news of good deeds. A stranger paying a neighbour's unfair fine; a colleague's daughter raising funds to help her grandmother's fight against cancer; a hiker rushing to the aid of a stranger being attacked by a bear…. For all of the sad news, it's important to remember the extraordinary reach of good-hearted citizens, behaviour that far outweighs the evil in this world, but attracts far less attention.

Newscasts routinely saturate the airwaves with devastation and loss, and then end the broadcast with a cute animal or kids' story. It's not enough. This fails to acknowledge the more heartening reality of everyday heroics: from big-picture movements like Doctors without Borders to groundbreaking daily gestures like Snow Angels or soup kitchen volunteers.

The reality is that as human beings, we do so much to stay connected. The failure is in not seeing this each and every day. I thought of this when I joined my children as they hunted Pokémon via a new app that revolutionized how gamers connect. The game was billed as forcing people to leave their homes, to walk their neighbourhoods, to reach out to fellow travellers.

I read recently about a stand of genetically identical trees in Utah's Fishlake National Forest. It stretches over 100 acres, with 47,000 stems and a genetic legacy that is possibly a million years old. It is described as the largest connected organism on Earth. Nonsense! Human beings are the largest connected organism on the planet: it is our duty to remember this and to reach out to others, with every breath we take. This, surely, is Christ's message. Do unto others. What a concept.

A Mediator for Humanity

And Mary said, "My soul magnifies the Lord."
Luke 1:46-47

The 100th anniversary of the apparition of Our Lady of Fatima in 2017 marked a celebration of one of the most dramatic accounts of apparitions in our time. Beginning with three visits by the Angel of Peace in 1916, three shepherd children in Portugal claimed to see the Virgin Mary via six apparitions ending on October 13, 1917. Our Lady promised to reveal three secrets to the children, and offered a miracle upon her last visit, which was witnessed by more than 60,000 people. One of these secrets is said to have predicted the attempted assassination of Pope John Paul II in 1981. Lucia Dos Santos, the eldest of the three children, later saw an apparition of the Child Jesus and the Virgin Mary in her convent room in 1925.

Dating back to the 1500s, the Anglo-French word *aparicion* references the Epiphany as an opening of Heaven to the world. Just as the revelation of the Christ child to the three magi offered a glimpse of a greater glory, so an apparition can be understood to open a door to divine understanding. Over time, the word has come to be used as a signifier of anything ghostly and unexpected, but it can be traced back to holy origins. Marian apparitions, in particular, occupy a unique place in the Catholic faith, and pilgrimages to major sites in Lourdes, Guadeloupe or even Medjugorje are legendary.

As important as the visions themselves, however, are the messages Mother Mary is said to have brought: from requests to build churches to prayers to end a world war. The visions all reveal a call to hope, though they also warn of challenges and crises, for which faith is offered as a refuge and an antidote. A particular feature of Marian apparitions is the disclosing of secrets that tell of impending tragedies or momentous events. In the end, though, such apparitions are powerful reminders of our belief in Mary and her place as a mediator for humanity—a bridge to our Lord.

As a university named in her honour, St. Mary's understand-ably looks forward to the month of May, which is traditionally seen as Our Lady's month. As Marge Fenelon, writing in *The National Catholic Register* in 2016, put it, "The idea of a month dedicated specifically to Mary can be traced back to baroque times. ... It was in this era that Mary's Month and May were combined ... with special devotions organized on each day throughout the month. This custom became especially wide-spread during the nineteenth century and remains in practice until today." For many, however, myself included, every day is Mary's day: a time to celebrate a blessing of incredible mystery and approachability. As St. Josemaria Escriva once said: "When you see the storm, if you seek safety in that firm refuge which is Mary, there will be no danger of your wavering or going down."

The Sweater

*"... because you have torn your clothes and wept before me,
I also have heard you, says the Lord."*

2 Kings 22:19

L et me confess that I am someone who tends to wear his clothes until they virtually fall apart. My favourite pair of shoes is over 10 years old, and my sweaters weren't much younger; most are pitted with an assortment of tears, holes and other character-defining features. In fact, it wasn't until I had a business meeting and noticed one of the attendees fixated on my shredded sleeve that I decided, finally, to replace them.

My first thought for the fate of my trusty companions was a quick burial in the trash. But as the mercury fell dramatically, it occurred to me that perhaps a faded or well-worn sweater was better than none, and so I dropped them in the local charity bin. I won't lie. My heart skipped a little at seeing my trusty steeds put out to pasture, but at least, I reasoned, it was a noble retirement.

As is often the way, however, I thought of those clothes going out into the community and wondered whose home they would join. Would they find their way to a cool retro-hunter keen to show off his thrift-shop chic? Would they be part of a workman's casual wear, perfect for odd jobs around the house? Or would the charity determine that they weren't fit for duty after all?

Recently, while I was volunteering at a soup kitchen, a remarkable thing happened. As I moved through the crowded hall, I noticed an older gentleman shuffling forward. He set himself up at a crowded table and wriggled out of his threadbare jacket. To my surprise, I saw that he was wearing one of my discarded sweaters. I recognized the torn sleeve, the holes peeking out beneath the armpits, and the frayed edges all around. I couldn't help but move towards him, and when he saw me he smiled. "Check out my new threads," he said, rubbing his sleeves happily. "Looking good," I answered, humbled and abashed. "Yes," he laughed emphatically. "Yes, I do."

If there are such things as life-defining moments, then that was surely one of them. I will never again take my good fortune for granted, and I will always remember that all gifts matter, be they large or small. More importantly, I know that I must go out into the world to offer service. Not just to render good to others, but because my soul needs feeding, and there is no greater meal.

The Strength of Brokenness

You shall break them with a rod of iron,
And dash them in pieces like a potter's vessel.

Psalm 2:9

At a panel presented by the remarkable Fresh Start Recovery Centre in Calgary, the executive director, Stacey Petersen, referred to the art of *kintsugi*, the Japanese practice of repairing broken pottery using silver, gold or platinum seams. The word *kintsugi* means "golden joinery," and this ancient technique reflects the art of lovingly repairing, rather than thoughtlessly discarding, damaged goods. If some struggled with a "philosophy of replacement" centuries ago, we can only imagine how much more prevalent such a culture of disposal is today, especially in the Western world. Everything, it seems, is expendable. If it's broken, out it goes!

Kintsugi pottery is remarkable to behold. It shows gold and silver cracks tracing through otherwise meticulous images on previously shattered cups, bowls and plates. It is a golden *craquelure*, or spiderweb, that holds divided and uneven pieces together. It is, of course, much more than simple repair work. The masterful artist does not simply restore but creates anew, often producing something more beautiful, certainly more intriguing, and at times even stronger than the item was originally.

I have always loved the story of the Persian carpet makers who introduced a deliberate flaw into all their masterpieces in acknowledgement that only God is perfect. And yet the concept of *kintsugi* seems much more accessible to the ordinary citizen, who is surrounded by, and indeed who may embody, damaged goods. Mr. Petersen drew the analogy between the recovering addict and *kintsugi* pottery, reminding us that beauty not only exists in, but is indeed created by, the reality of our imperfections and the struggle to improve, rebuild, renew. "We have all experienced brokenness: broken homes, trauma, broken hearts, broken relationships, lost loved ones.... None of us can escape the pain of being broken." But as he goes on to implore, "Reflect on your own life and notice how every crack has made you more beautiful, more resilient."

Kintsugi is a powerful metaphor for the art of healing: not just for the noble and heroic journey that addicts undertake in recovery, but also for all of us who bring our own doubts, imperfections and failures to the world around us, and where, through faith, family and friendship, we sometimes suture the chipped or broken pieces of our lives into something stronger and more beautiful. As Leonard Cohen puts it: "There is a crack, a crack in everything, that's how the light gets in."

The Strongest Stem

Its strongest stem became a ruler's scepter.

Ezekiel 19:11

The mace has been a staple of university ceremonies for over 600 years, with Oxford University first using one in the 16th century. Alternately a weapon of war and of diplomacy, the mace has been used in both parliaments and universities as the symbol to start proceedings, to ward off evil or to call people to attention. In the university context, it also represents the institution's authority to grant degrees, and as such, the mace-bearer always leads the procession of professors and students into the graduation hall.

One of the most exciting times for any university is convocation, when we have an opportunity to celebrate the achievements of our student community. Several years ago, St. Mary's University had the pleasure of awarding a record number of degrees, but also of presenting our new mace. The Rose Family Memorial Mace was crafted by the prestigious British firm of Thomas Fattorini, by appointment to Her Majesty the Queen, manufacturer of insignias and awards. The mace was designed and donated by one of our professors, Dr. Linda Henderson, to celebrate the university's 30th year as an educational institution.

The mace honours the achievements and spirit of the Rose family, including patriarch Harold Henry Rose, and Dr. Henderson's late sister Janet Rose, a pioneer in cartography and in the geomatics industry, whose company produced an extraordinary 3-D imaging map of our entire campus. It is for this reason that the mace includes a small compass rose on its finial. As our campus minister, Nancy Quan, pointed out at the dedication ceremony, a compass rose is "a directional keeper." It is a "harbinger of where we are going, and of the direction we want to take. A compass lets us know when we have gotten off track or when we have missed the mark. By orienting us, it helps us to look forward with purpose, but it wisely reminds us to keep looking over our shoulders to keep track of where we have come from. Where we come from does indeed matter. It shapes our vision."

The mace also features the St. Mary's star in several places, as well as our coat of arms. The design combines a hardwood staff with a hallmarked sterling silver head, a lucite stone in which floats the St. Mary's star, and it bears our university crest on two sides, enamelled in four colours and finished in 24-karat gold. Obviously, the rose, as the symbol of Mary our namesake, is important for us as a university. It also has a particular resonance to the Rose family, after whom the mace is named.

With our Rose Family Memorial Mace, along with our coat of arms and our new university flag, granted recently by the Chief Herald of Canada, St. Mary's is preparing to take on the next 30 years with renewed focus and purpose.

Artistic Designs

I have filled him with divine spirit, with ability, intelligence, and knowledge in every kind of craft, to devise artistic designs.

Exodus 31:3

I n Calgary, a recent unveiling of public art has reignited the debate on the value of taxpayer-funded projects. In particular, the launch of *Bowfort Towers*, a rusted metal and rock installation said to mirror the region's mountains and echo Blackfoot culture, has triggered visceral opposition. For some, the consultation with elders appears questionable and unlikely. Many are furious that the project went to New Yorkers when local artists are crying out for work; others balk at the $500,000 price tag when city arts groups are desperate for funding.

Many have countered that public art *should* be controversial and generate conversations, citing the fierce opposition to the Eiffel Tower as a case in point. As Don Braid pointed out, "In the late 1800s the Eiffel Tower project tore Paris apart. … Writers, painters, sculptors and architects vowed 'to protest with all our strength and all our indignation … against the erection … of the useless and monstrous Eiffel Tower.…'"

I will go out on a limb here and suggest that the latest Calgary project is unlikely to become a beloved cultural symbol for the city. And I will admit to a personal dislike of both the design and the cultural appropriation of the work itself. However, it would be a pity if a fraught work undermined an otherwise admirable initiative, which is to populate public spaces with art. Creative works entering the public domain are always important, not just as a trigger for healthy dialogue and conversation, but also as an acknowledgement of the power of art to transform society itself.

It is surely in recognition of this idea that so many of our Popes have spoken on the importance of art, including our last three pontiffs. For John Paul II, "Society needs artists ... who ensure the growth of the person and the development of the community." For Benedict XVI, 'Dear artists ... You are the custodians of beauty: thanks to your talent, you have the opportunity to speak to the heart of humanity, to touch individual and collective sensibilities...." And in speaking to the Patrons of the Arts in the Vatican Museums, a group whose work is dedicated to restoring treasured works, Pope Francis noted, "In every age the Church has called upon the arts to give expression to the beauty of her faith and to proclaim the gospel message of the grandeur of God's creation, the dignity of human beings made in his image and likeness."

It may be a stretch to suggest that public art lays claim to such lofty goals, but it shouldn't be. Every work of art opens a conversation that connects us to our shared humanity and reminds us of the need for beauty in a blighted world. As Pope Paul VI put it in 1965, "This world in which we live needs beauty in order not to sink into despair."

Persistence of Vision

The Lord does not see as mortals see;
they look on the outward appearance,
but the Lord looks on the heart.

1 Samuel 16:7

I have always been fascinated by film. Certainly, the spectacle of the big screen is exhilarating, and few of us in the Western world could claim to be ambivalent about the wonder of cinema. But my interest went beyond spectatorship. I discovered cameras at an early age and spent countless hours at my desk, out in the world, in darkrooms and in editing suites writing, filming, editing and making films. As a writer, film seemed to take the written word to another level, and despite the limitations and cost of early production processes, I always found a way to borrow cameras, buy expensive reels of film and coerce friends to play a role in one of my amateur movies.

While I loved the process of creating a world and then capturing it on film, I preferred the post-production process. First there was the exquisite wait as a reel of film was sent out for developing, a process that could take as long as a month, depending on the volume of work at the local camera shop. Then there was the screening of the raw footage, often shot out of order. My favourite part was assembling the strips of film into an order that told the tale. In my early university days, this could mean hanging thousands of numbered strips of 8- or 16-millimetre film around my room, and then agonizingly reassembling them, hand splicing them with tape until the movie was complete. Once, after meticulously assembling a movie over a two-week period, I watched in horror as the rickety university projector devoured my only copy in less time than it took me to cross the room and switch it off. Such were the joys, and pains, of film in the pre-digital age.

Later, as an academic, I began to work with the metaphor of film. One of my early books played with the concept of persistence of vision, a contested theory of how light was said to "burn" an image onto the retina long enough for the next image to replace it, thereby ensuring the effect of motion in the mind's eye. I worked with Aboriginal communities in Australia, for whom film had once been an invasive material said to steal the soul, and with modern Indigenous filmmakers who reappropriated film technologies to counter the harmful clichés that cinema had created around First Nations cultures. Film could be pablum, or it could be life-changing.

Recently, I have been thinking of film in the context of faith. On the one hand, it is true that the Bible has been the direct source of countless movies. Faith-inspired works add up to an even greater number. But film, too, as a technology, can be understood as a metaphor for faith itself. In film, like faith, we can understand the process of perception, of capturing an image and rendering it into meaning. An image, like faith, might emerge from a darkroom, and develop before our eyes, from nothing into something. Or it might emerge full of spectacle and light, then be edited through our faith life, made sense of, so that the enormity of a divine truth is somehow made comprehensible. But a film, like faith, is always greatest when it shines a light on an inner truth. A film, like faith, can be all spectacle and no substance, or it can be deep and layered, open to continuous understanding. In that sense, true faith is always more than meets the eye.

The Accent of God

The Lord confused the language of all the earth.

Genesis 11:9

As someone who grew up between languages, I have always been fascinated by the idea of translation. With a father who didn't speak English and a mother who didn't speak French, I was a verbal bridge between them for a very long time. Admittedly, in the course of their marriage they learned to mangle each other's language, yet it remained true that I largely spoke only French with my dad and English with my mom, and Franglais when they were together. "Can you pass *le sel*?" I'd say, or "*La poutine* is great!" Unilingual friends often felt at sea at my place. "It was like being on the border of two countries," a classmate once grumbled, "and not belonging in either."

Perhaps because of this, I have always been fascinated by the section of Genesis that describes the building of the Tower of Babel. According to some, the tower was built as a safeguard against a second flood, demonstrating humanity's attempt to second-guess or outwit the Lord. In anger at this arrogance, the Lord "confused" the languages of the earth. When I was a child, though, the story was an almost physical emblem of the tensions in the community between English and French in Montreal, and a fabulously logical example of the power of language to divide.

Over time, though, I began to look at this in another way. The formation of the languages created the world in all its magnificent diversity. After the Lord eliminated a common tongue, he "scattered" the people "abroad over the face of all the earth" (Genesis 11:9). Could it be, I wondered, that God wanted to test how human beings might find better ways to communicate at a deeper and more substantial level by removing the easy tools of speech?

Certainly, for my parents, language was eventually no boundary at all. Through love, they learned to hear each other for decades until their deaths. Since then I have comforted myself with the thought that the Word is about the importance of communication and translation. And I remind myself that for the Bible itself—however translated, in whatever language or form—the essence of the work is deeper and more mysterious than we can ever fully comprehend. And so understanding must always be a journey.

I asked my mom once if the mystique of my father disappeared as she learned his language. "No," she answered shyly, "because his accent always reminds me of that other world." Perhaps, in the end, that's what we should always listen for whenever the Bible is read: the echo of a greater mystery—call it the accent of God—which is always compelling and just out of reach. For that reason, faith must always be actively pursued rather than passively received. That, surely, should be clear in any language.

Stairway to Heaven

Singing and making melody to the Lord in your hearts.

Ephesians 5:19

Among church bloopers, this was always one of my favourites: "8 new choir robes are currently needed, due to the addition of several new members and to the deterioration of some older ones." This was only marginally more reassuring than the church bulletin that announced, "Today's sermon: How Much Can a Man Drink? With hymns from a full choir." For as long as I can remember, music has been a part of my churchgoing experience. As a young boy, I marvelled at the power of Gregorian chant, and specific hymns always made my heart sing. But it was our parish priest who helped me connect my own experience as a youth with the possibility of faith life, albeit through a failed experiment. I will never forget the day the priest hired a few of my friends to play what was ominously billed as the Electric Mass that left an entire congregation deaf for hours. I don't think the priest ever imagined that "Amazing Grace" could be filtered through the heavy metal electric guitar riffs of Metallica.

In a book on St. Francis of Assisi by Lawrence Cunningham, I was surprised to read that in his misspent youth the saint had an "interest in subversive music." The author noted that Francis loved French *chansons* in particular, which in the 1100s meant songs about love and frolicking, war and heroic deeds. This got me thinking about the role of music, both within and outside of faith, but also the ways that music has often both defined and defied "suitable" behaviour. As a young man, I remember my mother looking sourly at my interest in The Rolling Stones, and yet, not much earlier, she, like so many, had swooned over Elvis, so provocatively inappropriate at first that television stations refused to show him below the waist.

Music, youth and counterculture have always been linked. What appears scandalous now will surely be condemned as bland and dismissed by the next generation. But music, beyond this overly simplistic equation, abides. And it has been a deeply connected and controversial part of faith life as well. Mozart's famous adaptation of Handel's *Messiah,* for example, so hated when first performed, is now unquestionably associated with sacred times and rightly understood to be a masterpiece. As J.S. Bach once noted: "Where there is devotional music, God is always at hand with His gracious presence."

The Second Vatican Council and the Sacred Congregation of Rites specifically addressed the importance of music in liturgy in *Musicam Sacram*, where we are told that there is nothing "more religious and more joyful in sacred celebrations than a whole congregation expressing its faith and devotion in song." Clearly, they never heard me caterwaul. And while anyone listening to my teenage efforts to play "Stairway to Heaven" on the guitar would have run for the hills, for the most part music can be an enabling force, a community builder and a pathway to spiritual understanding, even when we're not all singing from the same song sheet. So, as St. Paul puts it, "Be filled with the spirit" and sing a song of praise.

The Biophilia Hypothesis

All things came into being through him.

John 1:3

Thanks to generous donors, St. Mary's University in Calgary was able to complete the restoration of our water tower. Built by the Sisters of Providence in 1921, the tower has stood over the Midnapore site for nearly a century, its fortunes waxing and waning ... mostly waning ... over time. As a wooden structure built when metal towers were coming into prominence, the tower has fallen prey to wildlife, inclement weather and the simple reality of aging. It was stabilized and cleaned, and then, for decades, left to wither away. Recently, however, we were able first to transform its imposing 80-foot exterior, and then to fully restore the glorious interior, creating what is arguably the most remarkable boutique art gallery in the country.

As we stood inside the renovated space, I commented that I felt an extraordinary sense of peace. It truly felt as though the cares of the world could not penetrate the walls. As soon as I said this, I looked around sheepishly, fearful that I'd be labelled as a kook, but instead everyone was nodding. Our conservation architect spoke first. "Have you ever heard of the Biophilia Hypothesis?" he asked. "It's a well-known theory that human beings need to be connected to the natural world." Like all academics, I immediately began to research the phenomenon.

There is nothing more exciting than someone putting a concept around something long experienced. And so it was with E.O. Wilson's biophilia hypothesis and our need to "affiliate with other forms of life."

We are all familiar with understanding experience through phobias—the fear and aversion we have to myriad forces in our world. Less common is the tendency of seeing our world through philias—the positive energies and attractions we might feel, as human beings, for the natural world. And biophilia speaks to this. In its wider sense, of course, the hypothesis posits an understanding of our human connection with other fauna and flora. Just as fascinating to me is the concept of biophilia as it connects to conservation. Here the argument is that human beings will be more connected to restorations and developments that incorporate organic materials and the natural world—what is often referenced as a major component of sustainable design and green architecture. Clinical evidence has shown that immunological and neuro-endocrine systems improve in patients who are connected, in some way, to the natural world.

Is it a stretch, then, to feel this same energy in a building whose sole purpose was to supply water to a home for the aged and orphans, and whose remarkable natural timbers bear the marks of woodpeckers and mice? Is it crazy to think that the deep, rich smell of wood that suffuses the towering space is somehow healing and protective? In *Laudato Si'* (On Care for Our Common Home), Pope Francis, citing his namesake, reminds us that there is an "integral ecology" and an "inseparable bond" between concern for nature, justice for the poor, commitment to society, and interior peace. Surely conservation is part of that remarkable equation, and the tower a small but powerful symbol of that connective tissue.

The Untouched Garden

They shall flourish as a garden

Hosea 14:7

My children always tease me for being a workaholic, and they roll their eyes whenever I have time off. "Get ready for the special projects," my daughter announces melodramatically. "Dad, you suck at relaxing," my son will confirm. They're right, of course. For whatever reason, my brain wants to fill the empty space. At worst, I see unused time as a deficit, at best as an opportunity to get things done. I'm told that this is a common psychological reality for many. In a doctor's waiting room, many will fidget, search their phones or pore over magazines without seeing their content, just to fill the gap.

In art there is a theory called *horror vacui*, from the Latin "fear of empty space" or the Greek "fear of the empty." The term essentially describes movements where artists felt the need to fill every inch of canvas. Examples of this include ancient Arabesque Islamic art, illuminated manuscripts like the *Book of Kells*, and many of the works of the Victorian age. Jean Duvet's famous engravings immediately come to mind, where every inch of the image is covered in exquisitely etched lines. Perception, of course, works the same way, with the brain often filling in missing pieces of a picture, or a memory, and then completing it in the mind's eye—whether it is there or not.

I thought of this, strangely enough, when rereading Pope Francis's *Laudato Si'*, and this time I was struck by his reference to St. Francis's insistence that "part of the friary garden always be left untouched, so that wild flowers and herbs could grow there, and those who saw them could raise their minds to God." "Epiphany" is too strong a word for this, but I thought immediately of this compulsion so many have to fill all so-called empty space—in time, in landscape, in conversation—and realized that I have been mistaking the nature of these open spaces.

Many will be familiar with the notion of fallow land: usually those parts of a farm that are left untended after successive years of cultivation. One of the dictionary definitions for fallow land is "obsolete"; another is "dormant." Both seem far from what is actually happening in the soil. In reality, fallow fields allow the soil to rebuild its nutrients and recover fertility. The land isn't dormant—it is coming alive!

Perhaps this is a lesson available to all of us—that we do not need to cultivate every inch of unfilled time and space in our lives. It is okay to stop, and pause, and even to do nothing in order that our psyches can replenish, and in the stillness hear the voice of God. Maybe that is the special project I should be looking forward to. The garden is already there: I just have to leave it alone and watch the grass … the wildflowers … grow ….

A Feast of Doubt

"Do not doubt but believe."

John 20:27

There is a charming drawing by pastor and cartoonist Joshua Harris where St. "Doubting" Thomas laments to his fellow disciples: "All I'm saying is we don't call Peter, 'Denying Peter', or Mark, 'Ran away naked Mark'. Why should I be saddled with this?" His colleague replies, "I see your point, Thomas, but really, it's time to move on."

The Feast of St. Thomas offers one of the more reassuring moments in faith formation. Often, when we think of martyrs and saints, I hope it's true to say that we are occasionally overwhelmed and abashed. How often do we read a heroic tale of faith within persecution and wonder: "Would I be as strong?" or "Would I pass the test?" It is surely true to say that all of us have moments of doubt, of weakness, of insecurity. Few would feel they truly measured up to the benchmark set by God.

Thomas, for many, is both the hope within weakness and the fragile person's source of envy. Not only did he get to walk with Christ, but also, when he doubted, Jesus himself provided the answer to his prayer. "Put your finger here and see my hands" (John 20:26). How often have we cried out, at times of weakness, "Show me a sign"? For most, it is only a quiet faith, through prayer, that has followed the request.

Pope St. Gregory the Great noted that "Thomas's unbelief has benefited our faith more than the belief of the other disciples; it is because he attained faith through physical touch that we are confirmed in the faith beyond doubt." St. Gregory goes on to say, "The Lord permitted the apostle to doubt after the resurrection; but He did not abandon him in doubt." These two factors are of the most significance to me: that doubt is not cause for abandonment, and that Jesus is always ready to receive us. It takes the pressure off our imperfections, but remains an incentive to be better.

This is one of the remarkable opportunities that a Catholic university offers, and makes available, to its community. The goal of higher education is to pursue faith and reason; to explore and to doubt; to journey and to discover. It was never the goal for Jesus that his disciples follow blindly. Indeed, he insisted that they question in order to understand. He never feared the difficult question or shied away from a challenge. Similarly, universities—especially Catholic universities—must never censor inquiry. They must pursue discomfort to seek and achieve the truth honestly. As Jesus himself put it, "Blessed are those who have not seen and yet have come to believe" (John 20:29).

Hamster Sandwiches

For all of us make many mistakes.

James 3:2

O ne of the biggest transformations in today's culture is in the level of technological change that has made life not only easier, but also faster. I'm thinking in particular of the way information has been digitized, so that content can be written, designed or laid out, edited and converted into final form almost instantaneously. As a long-time editor, I can remember when a laboriously typed manuscript had to be sent to a typesetter, which was then returned as galley proofs, which we hand corrected to return for inputting and reprinting. I'm also old enough to remember the invention of the self-correcting tape on the IBM Selectric typewriter, which was considered a miraculous time saver. When the personal computer came along, with a floppy disk that could hold the equivalent of a long email, it was downright revolutionary. My son put this in perspective when he informed me that my iPhone 5 had more computing power than all of the machines that guided a rocket ship to the Moon in the 1960s.

In an imperfect world, mistakes are inevitable, but it is certainly true that with speed comes an increased likelihood of errors. As I was rushing to complete a truckload of paperwork before the Christmas break, my assistant sent me a classic typo:

a motion thanking retiring Board members for their "mangy contributions" to the university. (Luckily she caught the mistake in time and substituted "many" for "mangy.") As readers of my column know, I wasn't so fortunate when I sent a note to my faculty with the salutation "Dead Colleagues." Another friend told me of her frustration with an email option to "recall" an email that had the effect of drawing attention to the error-filled email she had sent. People who would normally delete the email unread found three versions of the text instead—the original, the retracted and the corrected—and gleefully dwelled on all the mistakes.

In the end, of course, and irrespective of the technology, human error will always find a way to make its voice heard. One of my favourite transpositional mistakes was from the 1980s, when Gary Larsen was publishing his cartoon *The Far Side*. In one newspaper it appeared next to *Dennis the Menace*, each a single panel with the humorous caption typed at the bottom. On at least one occasion, typesetters accidentally printed the punchlines under the wrong comic. In a classic blunder, Larsen's cartoon showed a cranky young snake at the dinner table saying, "Lucky I learned to make peanut butter sandwiches or we woulda starved by now," while Dennis Mitchell complained, "Oh brother ... Not hamster sandwiches again!"

In the university context, especially in the pedagogical sphere, errors are the basis of learning. I remember one student telling me that they were bilingual in at least three languages before submitting an essay that proved they were literate in none. Another insisted that she was a work alcoholic and therefore not afraid of studying. In both cases they went on to become A students. We can't be afraid of our mistakes, and just as importantly, we need to be able to laugh at ourselves, not take things too seriously, and then strive to improve. As John Powell once said: "The only real mistake is the one from which we learn nothing." Or to quote Andrew Mason, "Admit your errors before someone else exaggerates them." After all, as one of the above students succinctly explained when I corrected her work, "To air is human!"

Like Sand Through the Hourglass

So Joseph stored up grain in such abundance
—like sand of the sea—
that he stopped measuring it; it was beyond measure.

Genesis 41:49

One of the realities of the 21st century is the awareness that what might have once seemed infinite is limited. For those of us who are older, we know this about our own passing days, learned sadly through the loss of loved ones. The indestructibility of our youth gives way to a recognition of our own mortality. But it is true as well that we look to the world's flora and fauna and see species vanishing at an alarming rate. Droughts remind us not only how precious water is as a commodity, but also how quickly it can disappear. It had never occurred to me, however, to consider one of the world's most precious commodities, which is likewise disappearing: sand.

As an article in *The New York Times* pointed out, "we use more of this natural resource than any other except water and air"; it goes on to remind us that sand is the basic ingredient in every road, shopping mall and office tower that we build the world over. We stare through it every day, if we remember that glass often uses liquid sand as a major component. According to a United Nations report, enough sand was used in 2012 alone to build a 30-metre wall around the equator!

I remember once being in a developing country and watching as sand was removed from a desperately poor communal village waterfront and transferred to the rocky detritus of a beach facing a luxury resort. Several months later I stumbled across the rock-strewn beaches of Cannes and couldn't help but think of the irony. The reality, of course, is that this $70 billion industry is ravaging villages, coastlines and other sites to provide sand for the wealthy—and is slowly disappearing.

In one of the most impassioned epistles of our times, Pope Francis has reminded us of our responsibility to the environment. What is so powerful about the Pope's message in *Laudato Si'* is that it reminds us how the environment is not simply about pristine waterways. In fact, it speaks to our relationship to each other, and it underlines extraordinary relationships of power. Not surprisingly, those who are without power suffer most because of a damaged human and natural ecology. As the Pope himself argues, "The world's poor, though least responsible for climate change, are most vulnerable and already suffering its impact." In time, however, there will be nowhere to turn. The sands will flow through our fingers and be gone.

Soft Skills

And where is the place of understanding?
Job 28:20

I recently conducted several job interviews. The phrase "soft skills" appeared a number of times—occasionally from the candidates themselves, but mostly in written feedback from audience members. One respondent noted, "I'm delighted that candidate X has clearly demonstrated soft skills. She appears able to listen to others, to communicate effectively." When I first read through the feedback, I accepted this without a second thought. After all, a professor or an administrator in a liberal arts university frequently relies on such terms to define the importance of the work we do in the humanities.

"Hard skills" are often described as job-related tasks: woodworking for a carpenter, coding for an IT professional. This job requirement is then usually supplemented with skills that supposedly improve an applicant's desirability—soft skills such as interpersonal abilities, communication skills, creative thinking, and work ethic. Liberal arts institutions almost always make a point of celebrating these as a mark of distinction to prove the worth of their degrees, especially in an age that tends to diminish the importance of the arts. And I have been a part of the soft skills bandwagon. Until now!

It occurred to me recently, in writing one of the many speeches that I deliver as a university president, that the very thought of labelling interpersonal or communication skills, creative thinking and an ability to collaborate with diverse groups as "soft" is misleading, if not condescendingly wrong. There is nothing soft about encounter. There is nothing soft about listening well and bringing diverse viewpoints together. And there is definitely nothing soft about the ability to think creatively and outside the box by drawing on complex philosophies, theories and perspectives. On the contrary, these are the hardest skills.

A colleague once dismissed my work by stating sarcastically, "Well, you could never build a bridge." And I remember thinking, "Yes, I can, and I do: between traumatized stakeholders in Indigenous communities and the institutions that once oppressed them, between colleagues in competing departments, and between diverse and separated individuals and groups." Surely this matters as much as the physical infrastructures other disciplines provide. Indeed, it is only diplomacy and communication that connect a divided world—and we see all too often the result when these are lacking.

So the next time someone says something about mastering the soft skills, remember how very hard this is to do.

Sorry Not Sorry

"Forgive them; for they know not what they are doing."

Luke 23:34

O ne of the most repeated observations my children made about Canada after we moved here from Australia can be summarized in two words: "cold" and "apologies." Specifically, they simply couldn't believe that anyone could stay alive given the harshness of Canadian winters; and they couldn't believe how often Canadians apologized … for everything. The classmate who said sorry to the driver who accidentally backed her car into him was the extreme end of the absurdity. When my son asked him about it, the kid answered simply, "Reflex."

With this in mind I was surprised to discover a new movement sweeping the internet, arguably trans-border but still, an equally Canadian phenomenon. The best way to refer to it is as "Sorry not sorry." A quick search of the web tells us that SNS can be a passive-aggressive protest against needless apologies; against ridiculous statements; or indeed against anything where an apology might be expected but where the speaker feels it's unwarranted. There is even a song by Demi Lovato called "Sorry Not Sorry."

While the phenomenon has a nasty side for sure, and has been used as a not-too-subtle opportunity to protest against political correctness—Canada 150, colonization, racism, sexism, and so much more—it shouldn't be dismissed out of hand. In some ways the trend identifies pent-up frustration with self-expression at a time of hyper-monitoring of behaviour. More than any other generation, our children in particular have their lives and feelings filtered through social media—Facebook, Twitter, Instagram and more. The effect of this is that even half-serious, injudicious comments can hit the spotlight, and vast armies of internet trolls can then magnify an attack, making it the equivalent of front-page news.

In such a climate we need to remember that apologies are powerful tools for redress, and not simply lip service to political correctness. Acknowledging past wrongs—for example, residential schools or the impact of colonization—is not to dismantle or attack all the good that has also been accomplished in the nation. To say "remember" is not an invocation to forget. It is about creating stronger bonds, built on acknowledgement and partnership. The Bible reminds us of this time and time again. Even from the cross—especially from the cross—Jesus asks for forgiveness, so that we can be given hope. Sorry. Yes. *Sorry.*

Silent Night

A time to keep silence, and a time to speak.

Ecclesiastes 3:7

A friend of mine complained that he'd recently been to a retreat and that everyone had been standoffish. "No one would speak to me!" he wailed. I didn't have the heart to tell him it was a silent retreat. The first time I attended one of these, at the invitation of a dear friend now gone, I remember feeling a fair bit of anxiety about how I would cope. "You'll love it!" my friend reassured me. "Silence is golden. But we'll have to stay in the retreat annex." "Why?" I asked, waiting for the punchline. "So we can talk, of course." (He was serious.)

The fact is that silence, especially given our busy age, is an alien country for many, and at first it feels odd to visit there. Silence changes our relationship to space, to time and to others. At dinner, for example, you begin to hear the sounds of living: the chewing and swallowing, the clink of cutlery, the sound of breath. You tend, slowly, to look inward, so that eventually you move by others and see only shadows. There's no expectation that you will communicate, so eventually you relax and don't feel rude for not making eye contact. The real challenge is all the room your thoughts suddenly have license to enter. Here, it would seem, is the space where prayer and reflection can flourish.

Throughout the Bible, we are shown the importance of silence, even for Jesus! From Matthew to Mark to Luke, we are told of Christ's quest for solitude as a way to encounter God, and often as a way to cope with busy or traumatic times. After ministering to the sick, casting out demons, multiplying the loaves and fishes and after the death of John the Baptist: each time, Jesus sought solitude and prayer to process what he had experienced.

There can be no doubt that the voice of God is available to all—but the conflagration of sound that distracts, misleads and deafens is significant. It can make us deaf to Grace. As St. Mother Teresa once said, "We need to find God, and he cannot be found in noise and restlessness. God is the friend of silence. See how nature—trees, flowers, grass—grows in silence; see the stars, the moon and the sun, how they move in silence.... We need silence to be able to touch souls." For this reason alone, we should find the time to discover the sound of silence, because in it we can find a voice more powerful than words.

Fake News

"The truth will make you free."
John 8:32

I grew up believing that great journalism was objective and that newspapers had a mandate to present a balanced story, regardless of an individual journalist's personal position. When I scanned the headlines of *The National Enquirer* at the grocery checkout counter, there was always the comfort of knowing that it was exaggerated—that its contents were deliberately bogus. That was its brand, and there were many other such newspapers and magazines that specialized in lurid stories. So I knew not to take it seriously.

When I lived in Australia, a good friend who happened to be one of the most remarkable, and yet chronically underemployed, playwrights I knew was forced to work for a scandalous magazine to make ends meet. When I caught up with him one day, he looked especially depressed. He'd been asked to write a UFO abduction story to go with a salacious picture of scantily clad women that had been submitted to the magazine. "What am I to do with this?" he sighed, showing me the image. "They look very tanned," I pointed out helpfully. "Better say they were taken to Mercury."

The idea of objective journalism has always been a bit of a fiction, with newspaper barons changing the story to fit their political interests from as far back as Randolph Hearst, if not before. Yet it is still somewhat shocking to hear a president of a nearby nation describing live photographs of an event as fiction, or discrediting actual, even recorded, evidence as "fake news." While this is the basis of disinformation campaigns, especially during wartime, it's odd to see it done by one person about his own community. And the internet, with its various instruments of social media, helps this misinformation to proliferate.

I thought of this one year during the Bishop of Calgary's homily at St. Mary's University's End-of-Term Mass. Bishop McGrattan read from John 8 and discussed the famous interchange between Christ and the Pharisees. How interesting to read what seemed to be another dialogue about fake facts, and how refreshing to hear a speaker talking plainly about the unvarnished truth. "Very truly, I tell you..." (John 8:34).

This is a theme specifically picked up by Pope Francis himself, of course. In his message for World Communications Day in 2018, the Pope opens by reminding us that "Communication is part of God's plan." He labels fake news as the "spreading of disinformation" that turns the other into an enemy. More importantly, he reminds us that the antidote to hurtful lies is peace: "Peace is the true news." It's an important insight to which we should all pay attention. Or to put it in the parlance of the paperboys of yesteryear: "Extra! Extra! Read all about it!"

Whither the Truth?

*For considering the flood of statistics involved and
the difficulty there is for those who wish to enter upon the
narratives of history because of the mass of material,
we have aimed to please those who wish to read.*

2 Maccabees 2:24-25

In the Gary Oldman movie *Darkest Hour*, we are offered a glimpse into the complexity of leadership at a time of deep crisis. The story of Britain's near surrender to Hitler's seemingly unstoppable onslaught has been told many times over. This film adds to that narrative, not simply by offering the public a *tour de force* performance by the lead actor, but also by delving into the sheer weight of decision making when the lives of others are in the balance. To do this, we are shown a stumbling and unpopular Churchill choosing deliberately to lie to the British public, even against the counsel of King George VI. In an early speech on the BBC, Churchill disguises the bleak reality of the allies in their battle against Hitler. For Churchill, it is more important that the populace retain hope.

What is remarkable about this film is not so much its skillful, though modest, retelling of a historical moment, but rather the way it becomes a story about storytelling. The film ruminates on the importance, and the danger, of truth, while itself dissembling on the actualities of history. In what is possibly the most uplifting and inspiring moment in the film, we see Churchill evade his driver and descend, for the first time, into the Underground. Here, in a stalled carriage, he encounters the "ordinary" Briton—young and old, black and white, male and female—where the doubting prime minister, on the verge of surrendering to Hitler, is reminded that he—that Britain—must never surrender.

The fact that the moment underground never happened is relevant in some respects. Certainly, filmmaking, even documentary filmmaking, always takes liberties with the materials it chooses to use. But here we may legitimately ask: Is this ethical, given that the film explores the very issue of truth in storytelling? Alissa Wilkinson, writing for *Vox*, asks a key question about this film: "Should we fudge the truth, or represent fantasy as truth—without also explaining that it's fantasy—to inspire people to do right?" She then asks, "Where is the line between good storytelling and propaganda—and are the means okay if the ends are good?"

The answer to that question may lie in the old chestnut that "History is written by the winners." One could add that it is then reshaped and "improved" by Hollywood. Churchill's stirring speech, legendary in all respects, is shown to resolve conflicts and doubts, especially his own, that he may never have had. But when his opponents in the House witness the ovation at the end of his speech, one character asks, "What just happened?" to which a stunned Viscount Halifax replies, "He mobilized the English language, and sent it into battle." One of the best quips never said, and arguably one of the best closing lines in film—ever.

Darkest Hour is a film about stories. It speaks to the need of human beings to be inspired, to have hope, to believe. Surely there is some irony—especially in our era of fake news—in the fact that this eloquent elegy to honour in truth telling is predicated on the need to fabricate. Or is this just too simplistic? Is it asking of art something we shouldn't? In the end, if a story moves us and gives us hope, does it really matter how it did so? I would like to think it does.

The Voice of the Church

With many golden bells all round,
to send forth a sound.

Ecclesiasticus (Sirach) 45:9

Recently, my daughter and I were driving to our local church when we noticed that virtually all the townhouses were for sale. This is a common phenomenon for these particular residences, and I commented that they must be particularly flawed to be repeatedly relisted. My daughter suggested that perhaps it was the bells. "It would be hard to live next to a church with the bells ringing at all hours of the day or night." I shook my head. "They don't do that anymore," I assured her. "Three times a day, max, and usually only on Sundays." "And for special occasions," she added wisely.

Church bells have been associated with spiritual observance since Paulinus of Nola first introduced them in 400 AD. Pope Sabinianus officially sanctioned their use in 604 AD. Some have claimed that they were a response to the Muslim practice of *adhan*, or the call to prayer. No matter how they began, innumerable uses and practices related to bells have evolved as Christian traditions. Most often, the bells signal the beginning of the church service, or ring out the old year and herald the new. It was once the case that the bells would peal on the hour and the half hour, or to mark a wedding or a funeral.

It is hard to imagine, in our time of automation, that entire communities exist to bring the bells alive. Campanologists study the technology of bells, and often oversee the rather complex and extensive variety of bells used in churches throughout the world. Bell ringers, meanwhile, are the hands-on people, stereotypically represented by the figure of Quasimodo in Victor Hugo's *The Hunchback of Notre-Dame*. One particularly charming cartoon shows an exhausted group of bell ringers, tangled in their ropes, with a priest commenting, "Well, that's the last time we do *Flight of the Bumblebee*."

The reality is that the ringing of the massive church bells is an art, with over 40,000 professional bell ringers working in England alone. Complex styles of bell ringing have emerged over time, including Bolognese, English and Veronese full-circle ringing. In Russia, a concerted effort was made to rescue the dying art of bell ringing in the 1960s, so that today there are numerous experts in the field. And of course, the bells have played a remarkable role in literature, announcing the death of loved ones, hope and the end of war, and celebrating new life. Given their history, it is difficult to believe that anyone might object to them.

In fact, though, the bells are under siege. A recent article announced that the bells of St. Mary's Church in Ashwell, England, would be silenced. They had chimed every 15 minutes for 117 years! A quick scan of the internet showed that this silencing phenomenon is growing. A noise abatement ruling in Sandwich saw the St. Peter's Church bells "curfewed" due to a single resident complaint. Churches throughout the United States have been subjected to court challenges for noise pollution. It reminds me of Ezra Pound's comment that the "act of bell ringing ... implies the pointless interference with the quiet of other people." Not surprisingly, numerous campaigns worldwide have also seen residents protest against the silencing of the bells. For so many, the bell tower issues a welcome "joyful noise" (Psalm 66:1).

As a child, I lived across the street from our parish church, and it was certainly true that the Sunday call to prayer was impossible to ignore. But for me the sound was magical. It was a sign of faith, certainly, but also of community. It reminded me that I was never alone, and that something greater than myself stood near, always watching over me. As Henry Wadsworth Longfellow once wrote, "… bells are the voice of the church; They have tones that touch and search the hearts of young and old." We do well to heed their call.

What Profits the Whole World?

Do my prophets no harm.

Psalm 105:15

"For what will it profit them to gain the whole world and forfeit their life?"

Mark 8:36

I have to admit that I was not the sharpest tool in the shed when it came to my faith life. I did tend to take things quite literally. In part it may be because I was a true bilingual hybrid, with a Francophone father and an Anglophone mother, neither of whom spoke the other's language until late in their marriage. So I translated. A lot and badly. Sometimes opportunistically.

If my parents were arguing and my mother let out a string of complaints, my dad would turn to me for a translation, *in media res*. My account usually went like this: "Mom says that even though she disagrees with what you're saying, she finds it hard to concentrate when your deep blue eyes meet hers." He would usually pause, in confusion, and his reply would be somewhat softened, which I would translate thusly: "I hear what you're saying but your beauty is disarming me." Then I would quietly leave while they were kissing and making up.

I was less in control during Mass. Homonyms always left me struggling. In one particular service, the reading was from Mark:

"For what will it profit them to gain the whole world and forfeit their life?" The homilist, rather inconveniently I thought, then spoke about the prophets. Maybe a reference to Luke 4:24 (I'm probably conflating two homilies): "Truly I tell you, no prophet is accepted in his hometown." I knew a thing or two about business! My dad always aimed to make a profit and people sure liked him in our neighbourhood. Then again, that was mostly because he extended credit to anyone who couldn't pay him, which is why we were desperately poor. So perhaps we didn't make a profit! It was incredibly confusing.

When I raised my confusion about the words, my mother became somewhat exasperated in trying to set me straight. She patiently explained the difference between "profit" and "prophet." When she was done, it seemed to me that the terms were opposites. One was all about gain, and the other about giving: advice, warnings, charity and so much more. I thought of this recently in reading an article in *The Catholic Register* by scripture scholar Scott Lewis, SJ, who noted that "True prophecy is the fruit of humble prayer, a compassionate heart and meeting God in the silence." He went on to say, "A true prophet is always willing to pay his or her dues, suffer the consequences of the mission and does not revel in the status of victim. Most of all, the words of the prophet should always give hope and courage to the broken-hearted, oppressed and wavering."

Giving versus taking. Compassion versus calculation. Love versus greed. In retrospect, it all makes sense. The harder road is the one of compassion, but it's the one we need to choose. That, it seems to me, is what profits the whole world.

Paralyzed Chickens

Do not speak in the hearing of a fool,
who will only despise the wisdom of your words.

Proverbs 23:9

I've written before about mondegreens, that wonderful phenomenon in language where a misheard phrase is substituted for the real thing, usually in music. Two such examples of this are from Pink Floyd's "Another Brick in the Wall," one line of which some listeners hear as "ducks are hazards in the classroom," and Eddie Money's classic line: "I've got two chickens to paralyze." (Substitute "dark sarcasm" and "two tickets to paradise" to get the original words.)

Classrooms are also rampant with misunderstandings, though perhaps none as cute as the one from a Bible studies class, where an elementary student explained that the epistles were the wives of the apostles. An in-class survey of elementary schoolchildren revealed the following: "Christians should only have one spouse. It's called monotony." Or: "Noah's wife was called Joan of Ark." My favourite was the child who claimed that Solomon had 300 wives but 700 porcupines! Cohabitation can be prickly.

While these may be legitimate misunderstandings, I do sometimes feel that, in some matters, we only hear what we want to hear. There's a cute cartoon of an elderly couple where the wife complains to her husband that he only hears what he wants to hear, to which he replies, "Thanks, I'd love a beer." Selective hearing, though, is no laughing matter. It is the subject of management textbooks, media workshops and even psychological training manuals.

I think it's fair to say that there are many reasons for this widely shared trait. It may be that we simply don't want to take on a task that is being asked of us. It is often because the news we are hearing is threatening or upsetting. At times it is because we have already decided what an individual is likely to say, and so we hear what we expect. Indeed, in such cases, it matters little what the actual message is—we've determined our response well in advance.

Whatever the case, no conversation ever takes place in isolation. I have heard people say that they pray to God, but never hear back! I can't help but wonder if the reality is that they don't like the answer they're getting back. But selective hearing isn't only a deficit—it's also a positive. Think of professionals forced to work in crowded, noisy spaces. The first responder listening to a victim in the midst of chaos all around her; a crisis-helpline responder in a busy call centre. If you ask these people how they do this kind of work, their answer is always humble and straight to the point: practice.

Perhaps, in the end, prayer is the same. We need to learn to focus, to listen, to filter out the white noise in order to hear the voice of God. But most importantly, we have to be prepared for the answer we may not want. If we do this, then, in the words of Isaiah 32:3, "the eyes of those who have sight will not be closed, and the ears of those who have hearing will listen."

Ghost Phrases

And to dust shall you return.

Genesis 3:19

As a photographer, I always assumed my interests were odd. My preferred subjects were dilapidated buildings, rusted metals and abandoned spaces. I love detailed close-ups of ghost phrases—slogans and ads painted on crumbling surfaces that are still just visible to the eye, decades after the products were available. Driving through the countryside I would often pull over to photograph a collapsed shed, a rusted sign or a crumbling wall.

Given how strange I assumed my interests to be, imagine how surprised I was to be invited to put together an exhibition of these works for a gallery in Australia. And when a book was commissioned to bring these photographic images together—*Border Crossings: Words & Images*—I began to think that perhaps my interests weren't so odd after all.

Of course, with the proliferation of the internet, it is now easy to see that this interest is indeed widely shared. There are so many fine artists who choose crumbling structures as the inspiration for their art that instead we should wonder why this view is so popular. Perhaps, in part, it's because there is something organic about seeing a wooden barn blending back into the soil, its timbers returning to the earth. There is something strangely reassuring and natural about this cycle of life. It speaks, in a wider sense, to our own mortality.

It wasn't until I saw a beautiful photograph of an abandoned church in a ghost town in the US, however, that I started to connect the idea of these photos to a question of faith and loss. It occurred to me that perhaps the effect of transforming the demise of a structure into beautiful art is something of a metaphor for the power of faith to similarly help us recover from, and even accept, loss. I realize now that many of the photographs I took for that exhibition were shot in the wake of my father's passing, and many of the frames that I built for the images of dilapidated buildings were made from timbers from my father's shop. Strange how it can take a lifetime to put two and two together.

Pope Francis has spoken often of the need to mourn and the natural sadness that comes when we lose a loved one, but he reminds us always of the greater joy behind this loss—that death is a beginning, not an end. In the harsh moment of tragedy this can be difficult to believe. Our hearts are broken and the loss weighs heavily. But over time we come to see the gift of the one we've lost, and to see that their light continues to shine. And knowing that they have returned to life, and have experienced the ultimate encounter with our Lord, is something to celebrate. In a way, our loved ones are ghost phrases, etched on our lives—faded, but never lost. As Pope Francis has put it, "Our loved ones have not disappeared into dark nothingness: Hope assures us that they are in God's good and strong hands. Love is stronger than death."

Perhaps this is the attraction that such buildings have always held for me. They are a living testimonial to what we build, in earnest and good heart, here on planet earth, but a reminder, too, that there's a greater plan in place for all of us. In the end—there's that phrase again—we are all just ghost phrases upon the land-scape. And it is the measure of our good deeds, our influence or heart, that determines how the image of our time on this good earth will fade, or how fondly others will gaze upon it, refusing to let it go entirely.

Good Vibrations

They are like a dream when one awakes;
on awaking you despise their phantoms.

Psalm 73:20

Recently I came across the term "fauxcellarm," only to discover that "ringxiety," as it's also called, describes a tactile hallucination that is widely experienced by many of us in the community. Perhaps better known as phantom vibration syndrome, it refers to the sensation that many experience of their phone vibrating or ringing in a pocket or purse, even when it's not. The phenomenon was described by one columnist as "our mind or body" warning us that "we may have crossed a line in this 'always on' society of ours." I will be honest and say that this has happened to me, and I eventually had to turn off the vibrate option. It took several months, but the phantom vibrations eventually went away.

As soon as I read about this phenomenon, I found references to it everywhere. It turns out there's an expression for this, too—the Baader-Meinhof phenomenon—which is the phrase used to describe a "frequency illusion," or a sense that a series of coincidences is occurring around a similar situation, topic or idea. The label came from a reporter travelling through Germany who kept hearing unrelated references to a specific terrorist group, but of course there are many examples and a related concept: synchronicity. How many of us have thought about a person only to have them call us later that same day?

Part of the explanation for this is that the brain is always looking for patterns, and when it finds one we focus on it. You could call this selective focus; when more examples occur, it's a cognitive bias. For example, wherever I'm driving on the highway, my speedometer always seems to read 111. I'm pretty sure that I don't drive at that speed all the time. However, whenever I look down and see that number, it sticks in my head. But because I'm a really intelligent person I'm pretty positive that my speedometer reads 110 just before it gets to 111—every time!

The mind, it turns out, is a remarkable country, and it seeks to make sense of the continuously changing information that travels through it daily. The mind is just as powerful at cancelling out material that is too stressful or too overwhelming to hold. As a professor I experienced this frequently in my students, many of whom, even the brightest in the class, seemed to go blank during exams. It happened so often that I eventually came up with alternatives to ensure that talented individuals were not penalized because of anxiety.

This is a long-winded way of building up to the idea of faith, and yet hopefully relevant. Faith, it seems to me, works both ways. There are often accusations that believers "manifest" moments of awe through an act of sheer will; alternatively, we are often blind to the obvious because the thought of the divine, so closely connected, can be overwhelming, to say the least. To my mind, the sanest route to take is to be sensitive to those good vibrations, and to remember that they aren't necessarily imaginary. Sometimes God reaches out in mysterious ways and sends us reminders of his presence and his love. Then it is up to us whether we answer the call.

Note to Selfie

Pay close attention to yourself.

1 Timothy 4:16

Recently I Googled the term "selfie" and determined quickly that no further research into the matter was needed. What I found were endless varieties of scantily clad self-representations, with very little analysis about why anyone would transmit these images of themselves, or what the images were meant to suggest other than an easily accessible sexuality occurring in epidemic proportions (79 million images on Instagram alone fall into this category). I don't think it's what Bogart meant when he said, "Here's looking at you, kid."

Psychologists speak of the nature of the selfie as a potential for both self-empowerment *and* self-harm—a symptom of the need to exhibit a strong self-image, but alternatively also a manifestation of enormous peer pressure leading to potentially damaging and irreversible exposure. In her column "Our Gender, Ourselves," published in *Psychology Today*, Dr. Peggy Drexler summarizes this contradiction in an entry entitled "What Your Selfies Say about You": "On the surface, the trend is sort of affirming, if undeniably self-absorbed … And yet selfies are also a manifestation of society's obsession with looks and its ever-narcissistic embrace."

Self-portraits have a long and respectable history in art. It is difficult to think of Rembrandt without also invoking his many self-representations. The selfie, however, manifests in a place and time where the technology allows a proliferation of damning images in a way that exceeds the user's ability ever to manage and contain the results. And the technology is located in the hands of exceedingly vulnerable individuals whose judgment may not be as sophisticated as one might hope. Even for more mature individuals, the reality of the selfie is that it can replace lived experience. As Dr. Drexler noted, speaking of one woman's journey with selfies, "before she even noticed her increasing fixation with her own appearance ... was the fact that she was so busy controlling her image that she'd often miss the moment in real life."

Pope Francis himself has spoken about this effect, and has characterized it as a self-alienating process. He uses the example of an encounter with a group of young people. "I went to greet them and only a few gave their hand. The majority were with their cellphones saying, 'Photo, photo, photo. Selfie!' I saw that this is their reality, that this is the real world, not human contact. And this is serious. They are virtualized youths."

We may well want to ask ourselves why self-discovery—a pursuit from time immemorial—manifests in this way, rather than through, for example, a more reflective, more spiritual address. In part the question is disingenuous. For most, the intoxicating and immediate bedazzlement of today's technology is ready-made for self-gratification. We have lost the ability to reflect quietly, or to retreat more deeply by looking in, rather than looking out ... or even looking deeply at ourselves.

Education, dare I say, is one vehicle that might help us to expand our view—that can allow us to take the self and embed it back into the real world. Education compels us to measure our own experience against a wider frame. A resonant faith is another such opportunity—a way to look deep within, instead of only at the surface, so that we may have a more comprehensive view.

The Mysteries Chef

"Blessed are you among women,
and blessed is the fruit of your womb."

Luke 1:42

There is a funny story about an elderly woman saying the rosary, unaware that a painter is on a scaffold above her repairing the church ceiling. As she prays, the mischievous painter whispers, "This is Jesus speaking." The old woman ignores him until finally the painter, thinking the woman is deaf, shouts, "Hello! This is Jesus!" The old lady raises her eyes to the crucifix and answers: "Just a moment, my Lord, I'm talking to your mother!"

For several years now I have prayed the rosary daily, but I've never had a similar interruption. For those who may not have undertaken a full rosary, I can say that it is a very powerful and rigorous practice. The rosary is divided into four sets of mysteries containing five mysteries each, for a total of 20. Prayed in sequence through the week, they offer a magnificent encapsulation of the story of Jesus and Mary.

The Joyful Mysteries tell of the Annunciation through to the birth of Jesus, his presentation at the temple, and the finding of Jesus in the temple. The Luminous Mysteries tell the story of the revealing of Christ to the world, from his baptism in the River Jordan, to the wedding at Cana through to the Last Supper. The Sorrowful Mysteries narrate the Passion, from the agony of our

Lord in the garden, through his trial and carrying of the cross to Calvary, to his crucifixion. And the Glorious Mysteries tell of his resurrection and ascension into heaven, the descent of the Holy Spirit at Pentecost, and finally the assumption of Mary into Heaven and her Coronation as Queen of Heaven and Earth.

For me, the daily rosary started as a way to ground myself at a difficult time, and while it has proven spiritually heartening, I must admit that at times it was challenging to maintain this practice given the realities of life. If I was ill or returning from a long evening of work, it might be after midnight before I could turn to the rosary, a prayer that can take up to 30 minutes. Until one day I read an account of a woman whose mother urged her to say the Hail Mary as she baked! I loved that story.

It reminded me of Salman Rushdie's novel *Midnight's Children*, where one of the characters baked her emotions into whatever she prepared. Hence, if she were crying when she cooked, those who ate her food became sad. If she baked euphorically, those who sampled her cuisine felt uplifted. I couldn't help but think the same would happen if you prayed while cooking. And since my own culinary ability is at best rudimentary, I decided to build the rosary into my daylight hours instead: the decades recited during the ride to and from work (guaranteed to eliminate road rage); while exercising (rather rare, I'm afraid); or while doing household chores (rarer still). And often, of a Sunday, I arrive early at church and pray the rosary before the Mass begins. There are still times when it is late at night before I can say the rosary. But most of the time the rosary is part of the fabric of my day: reassuring, tempering, enlightening. How can you go wrong when 53 Hail Marys, 6 Our Fathers and a handful of other awesome prayers are part of your day?

And Another Thing

How very good and pleasant it is
when kindred live together in unity!

Psalm 133:1

I t is no secret that I love everything to do with language. Less well known is that my favourite character is the ampersand—&—that strange design that so often appears in book titles and which is another version of the word "and." It is also no secret that my favourite literary device is the mondegreen, that odd term which means a mispronounced or misheard phrase, most often witnessed in song lyrics.

What I didn't know was that the word "ampersand" was itself a mondegreen, a discovery that led me to delve into the amazing world of letters. In doing so I learned that there were once 27 letters of the alphabet, with the ampersand appearing last! According to blog.dictionary.com, "In the early 1800s, school children reciting their ABCs concluded the alphabet with the &. It would have been confusing to say 'X, Y, Z, and.' Rather, the students said, 'and per se and.' 'Per se' means 'by itself,' so the students were essentially saying, 'X, Y, Z, and by itself and.'" Over time, the blog points out, "'and per se and' was slurred together into the word we use today: ampersand."

In my university days I used to design posters for local theatre groups, and I always struggled to get all the words in. On more than one occasion I was able to use the ampersand as both a stylish and an economical character to space out the titles and design. But the ampersand also made note-taking quicker, and it became a visual style all my own in letter writing. I suppose because of this connection, I always secretly thought the symbol belonged to me alone. Until recently.

In writing this column I discovered that the humble ampersand has been used by many, and often for extremely diverse political purposes, from the title of a leftist cartoon strip to the name of a political consulting firm and even for Emory & Henry College in Virginia. It's also the name of a five-star hotel in London!

In spite of, or perhaps because of, all this, it seems fair to say that the ampersand celebrates—indeed embodies—connections. It is a visual reminder for us to listen and link ideas, even if they aren't easily held together. Perhaps this is the best we can hope for in a divided world: that we bring together sentences, ideologies and causes in a healthy tension, so that we can better understand other points of view. Perhaps this is one more way of thinking about Pope Francis's call for a "culture of encounter."

Blaming the Round-headed Kid

*But the goat on which the lot fell for Azazel
shall be presented alive …
that it may be sent away into the wilderness.*

Leviticus 16:10

It is no exaggeration to say that the Bible and Shakespeare account for a staggering number of sayings, expressions and, in today's parlance, memes. These in turn have influenced book titles, movie themes and everyday sayings. Recently I became curious about the origins of the word "scapegoat" (for reasons that will become clear shortly). I wasn't surprised to learn that it emerged via one particular translation of the Bible in 1530. I *was* stunned to read, however, that this word was initially a mistranslation of the word *Azazel*. (I'm sure I'm not the only one who put down their coffee and thought, "Wait, there's not even a passing resemblance to that word….")

In an early version of the Old Testament, *Azazel* was incorrectly translated as *ez ozel*, meaning "goat sent out." It is found in Leviticus (16:10), which speaks of one goat sacrificed for the Lord, and another released into the desert carrying away the sins of Israel. It is this phrase that William Tyndale translated into Latin as *caper emissarius* or "escape goat," later adopted by the King James Bible in 1611. Over time, "escape goat" became the more familiar "scapegoat," referenced every year during the

Day of Atonement, or Yom Kippur – the holiest day of the year in Judaism.

The concept of the scapegoat came to mind when I was reading an article in *Crux* entitled "A Remarkably Hands-on Pope Gets All the Credit—and All the Blame." In this article, John L. Allen Jr. makes the point that arguably no other pope in history has been as involved in the inner workings of the Vatican, or been as hands-on with policy, action and initiatives emanating from Rome. Allen notes that with previous popes, unpopular decisions could often be blamed on the "courtiers" around him. With Francis, however, the buck stops with him.

No one who has read the Pope's encyclicals or listened to his interviews, however, would be in any doubt that this is exactly how he wants it to be. A driving thread through Pope Francis's commentaries is that we should all take responsibility for our actions, our words, our thoughts, whether this has to do with climate change, acceptance of refugees or responsibility to the poor.

Former US president Dwight D. Eisenhower once said that the "search for a scapegoat is the easiest of all hunting expeditions." Physicist Stephen Hawking whimsically noted that "a person who smiles in the face of adversity probably has a scapegoat." And Charles Schultz, the comic genius behind *Peanuts*, had one character wryly note: "There's our excuse … we'll blame everything on the round-headed kid!" Not Pope Francis. No escape goats—or round-headed kids—for him. It's all about character and accountability, even in the darkest hour.

Beyond the Surface of Things

Be merciful, just as your Father is merciful.

Luke 6:36

There is a well-known joke about a court jester who deeply offends his king and is then sentenced to death. The entire court lobbies the king for mercy, and they are partially successful. The king refuses to commute the death sentence, but he allows the jester to decide how he will die. Without skipping a beat, the court jester says, "I'd like to die of old age, please!"

What exactly do we mean by mercy? When Pope Francis called for a Holy Year of Mercy, to begin on December 8, 2015, and conclude on November 20, 2016, what exactly were we meant to celebrate? The *Oxford English Dictionary* provides a number of definitions for this, including the most common one: the demonstration of forgiveness towards someone over whom we have power. Alternately, mercy is described as a relief from suffering. Ironically, phrases connected to mercy include mercy killing (the taking of a life) and a mercy dash (the saving of a life).

However we define it, we should know that an act of mercy is both a wonderfully selfish gift and an altruistic one. After all, mercy is a gesture of forgiveness, hospitality, inclusion or help, but one that is never one-sided: we give to ourselves when we give to others. Mercy should never be about power over others.

It should be understood as an opportunity to grow the soul through an exchange of grace. And surely that can be gifted by a child to an adult as much as from a doctor to a patient … or indeed, a jester to a king.

As Pope Francis himself has explained, "The Church must be a place of mercy freely given, where everyone can feel welcomed, loved, forgiven and encouraged to live the good life of the Gospel." He goes on to say, "The call of Jesus pushes each of us to never stop at the surface of things." And then again: "No one can be excluded from the mercy of God!" In *Evangelii Gaudium* (The Joy of the Gospel), where he uses the word 32 times, he reminds us that "God never tires of forgiving us; we are the ones who tire of seeking his mercy."

So it's hard to define what the Year of Mercy represented in its totality, but I know it included this much: a deep reflection on our failures to forgive; an invitation for an immediate but permanent undertaking to reach out to others; and an opportunity to understand our own need for mercy, even for self-forgiveness when needed. Now that was a tender mercy.

I Will Remember

"Remember that my life is a breath."

Job 7:7

The month of November witnesses a number of important observances, from All Saints' Day and All Souls' Day which begin the month, to Remembrance Day in the middle, to the start of Advent that usually closes out the month. All of these mark an engagement with birth, death and resurrection in some complex sense. November is a time of remembrance and expectation, a celebration of history and hope, marked in the secular and non-secular calendar through the honouring of our war dead on the one hand, and the anticipation of Christ's birth on the other.

As our campus minister at St. Mary's University once reminded us, however, remembrance isn't only about the past. November should also be a time when we call to mind those individuals who continue to shape our days through acts of kindness, courage or compassion: a caregiver, a parent or a teacher, for example. It is also an appropriate time to acknowledge the huge impact that charities have on community needs: one that is felt most acutely at this time of year. Inevitably, the tender mercies that a student volunteer displays by helping out at a soup kitchen is paid forward into the community at large: yes, it directly helps an individual in need; but I firmly believe it also echoes out into the community as a spirit of grace that touches and inspires others. Sometimes the impact of that kindness is immediate; sometimes it is not felt until years later.

I was reminded of this as I thought about my father, who struggled as a small business owner at a time when big box stores were going up everywhere. When my father fell ill, and then later still after he passed away, I was surprised by the many people who came forward with offers of help. It was only then that I discovered that for years my father had extended credit to people in the community, many of them Italian migrants who were similarly in need. He had forgiven debts even while our family struggled to pay our own.

In those cold days leading up to Christmas, as I laboured with my grief to accept his death, I was raised up by those who came forward with offers of food, flowers or a hug. And when an elderly Italian couple stopped me on the street of my old neighbourhood in that dark year to explain how my dad had helped them at a desperate time, I realized that grace, once born and given, never dies away. When they urged me, with a seriousness that I will never forget, always to remember how good a man he was, it was easy for me to say, "I will remember."

The Saints Have Us Covered!

Contribute to the needs of the saints.

Romans 12:13

It's been said that Catholics have a saint for virtually every situation, event or possibility. Some of the more unusual include a saint for fireworks, unattractive people and dysentery (Saints Barbara, Drogo and Smyrna, in that order)! Without being disrespectful, it is hard to imagine being the saint of hangovers, oversleeping or caterpillars, but yes, they do exist. There is even a patron saint of brewers (St. Arnulf of Metz). On the cool but strange side of the spectrum, St. Hubert of Liege is the patron saint of hunters—and protects people from the fear of werewolves, while St. Columbanus is the patron saint of motorcyclists. I will leave it to another time to muse on how St. Isidore of Seville, who died in 636 AD, is the patron saint of the internet!

For all of the more unusual saints, there are of course those most widely embraced and understood, from St. Valentine, St. George and St. Francis of Assisi to St. Joan of Arc. It's also fair to say that many saints are invariably connected to a particular culture, from St. Mary MacKillop in Australia, to St. Kateri Tekakwitha for Indigenous peoples in Canada, to St. Patrick in Ireland.

One of the most popular events at St. Mary's University in Calgary is our annual hosting of our September Ghost Tour, where we open the campus to the community, re-enact scenes from our history, and help to mark our anniversary. As president of a Catholic university, I often field questions from the media about why we are celebrating Hallowe'en, and I am always at pains to point out that we are, in fact, celebrating the stories of the institution's founding, and not the popular feast at the end of October.

As a child, however, I was always confused that Hallowe'en came before All Saints' Day, and I wondered how they were connected. I eventually learned of the rich thread that links All Hallows' Eve (October 31) to All Saints' or Hallowmas (November 1) to All Souls' Day (November 2), and I came to look forward to the celebrations acknowledging the saints that have transformed our faith life throughout the ages. Despite this long tradition, it remains a mystery to me how some saints have come to represent their particular attributes. Perhaps it's enough to know that whatever befalls us, the saints have us covered! And now, if you'll excuse me, I need to say a prayer to St. Francis de Sales, patron saint of writers and journalists.

Educating the Heart

Besides being wise, the Teacher also taught the people knowledge, weighing and studying and arranging many proverbs.

Ecclesiastes 12:9

In the hilarious television show *Mr. D.*, the titular character expounds a basic philosophy about teaching. "Mark the smart kid's exam first and use it as an answer key." He explains in another episode about the mentoring of practicum students—basically, throw them into the deep end and take a day off. In his standup routine he once told a group of teachers, "I saw a seminar recently: 'Engaging Students in the 21st Century.' It was cancelled. You can't engage them anymore! Teachers saying, 'I'm not going to that! That's impossible.'"

Of course, Mr. D. is not actually a role model for us as teachers, though in the way of great parody, he often builds on real situations to make his humour more identifiable. While all of us no doubt prepare diligently for each class, it's true to say that the workload for teachers is at times overwhelming. And teaching isn't just about the material anyway. As teachers everywhere understand, it's *how* you present information, and how you connect to your students, that can be the difference between failure and success. All this is compounded by the different learning needs and styles of the students themselves. Clarity for one individual can be gobbledygook to another.

For all of these reasons, I think that teaching is one of the toughest gigs on the planet. And yet the world over, masochists keep presenting themselves to take on this challenge. Why? I truly believe that many individuals turn to this remarkable profession because they want to make a difference in the lives of others.

Teaching in the context of a faith tradition can be even harder. We live in a secular society, and the dynamic messaging of today's technology, and the contradictory information that flows to our children, is overwhelming.

The Calgary Catholic Education Foundation is one organization that understands the challenge for both teachers and students. Founded in 2008, the CCEF is a charitable organization that raises funds for schools in need—innovative educational experiences, technology, literacy projects and educational environments that ensure no child is left behind. And once a year, on Catholic Education Sunday, the organization rallies to raise funds through parishes and the community to support over $150,000 of initiatives. I'm proud to say that one year our Bachelor of Education students played an active role in helping to promote the Foundation's objectives, and one of our Education students was on the CCEF's board of directors. Together we worked to ensure that the value of education—and Catholic education in particular—was widely received.

Our job is not just to educate, but also to do this with passion, so we can help students find their own passion. Aristotle once said, "Educating the mind without educating the heart is no education at all." To which I think we can all say: Amen!

A Living Hope

He has given us a new birth into a living hope.

1 Peter 1:3 (New International Version)

Many years ago, when I lived in Australia, I was excitedly preparing for a return home to Canada for Christmas. As an only child of parents who were struggling financially, I had managed somehow to choose what seemed to be the furthest place in the world that I could live. The cost of travel, especially in those days, was prohibitive. So the December trip was a big deal, and the chance to catch up with my folks, who were my best friends in all the world, was truly special. But a week before I was scheduled to fly home, I received a frantic call from my mother. "You need to come home now," she sobbed. "Your father's had a heart attack."

There is perhaps little need to explain how nearly impossible it was to change my flights at that time of year, the complexity of leaving my classes early, or the horrific journey that unfolded at a time when direct flights from Australia to Eastern Canada were non-existent. My trip home involved four separate flights, coincided with one of the worst snowstorms in Toronto's history (it grounded all planes), and necessitated my hiring a courier service to ship me from Toronto to Montreal. When Highway 401 was closed down, I convinced the driver to let me take the wheel: we wound our way through backroads, dodging roadblocks and police. I arrived, after a 56-hour journey, to discover my father on life support. He never recovered, and I was not able to say goodbye. Shortly thereafter, just before another Christmas, my mother would be diagnosed with cancer and would slip quietly though painfully away, but at least I was able to spend some time with her.

It is perhaps for this reason that whenever Christmas comes around, a very large part of me braces for an unbearable sadness. It has been mitigated, over the years, by the presence of my children, who unfortunately never got to meet their grandparents. But despite this, the sense of cheer, the sense of reunion, of family gathering, contrasts sharply with the sense of loss. It is not something that I ever speak about, and I am of course careful never to raise this with my kids. And yet, how many, like me, wear the memory of sad tidings that the event inevitably brings.

My faith life has always been the anchor at these times. Many write of the true meaning of the season and the importance of celebrating Christ's birth amid the onslaught of commercialization. For me this takes on a special significance. The birth of Jesus is a reminder of joy, both in the moment (the birth itself), but also in the long term (what it represents for our salvation). It is here that I can remind myself that my parents are not lost to me; that they have been saved and that I will be reunited with them. Our Lord's sacrifice is equally a reminder of what giving truly is—at a level and scope that no one else can ever undertake, and that we perhaps can only vaguely ever understand. But what a precious gift it is. For that we can be deeply thankful.

Our Righteous Deeds

Where are your acts of charity?
Where are your righteous deeds?

Tobit 2:14

Every year, St. Mary's University in Calgary puts together a volunteer contingent to support the Our Lady Queen of Peace Ranch, which organizes a massive charity event for children of low-income families. The Ranch makes everything from face painting to crafts, meals, presents and winter clothes available to the children and their families free of charge. As long-time volunteers for this event, my kids and I have always been uplifted and humbled by this initiative, and as a university president I am equally moved by the tremendous response our students make in volunteering. In some years, close to one fifth of the university student population has turned out to help for that one event alone.

Volunteering is an odd thing. In some ways it is deeply selfish. There's no question that we do good for ourselves in the process of doing good for others. In other ways, volunteering is deeply sad. In the context of social justice, volunteering is a necessary evil—something that is done because our societies are deeply unequal, and deeply flawed. Shelters, food banks, clothing bins: all of these exist because our society fails to deliver equity to all, and so volunteers are needed to meet a profound failure in our culture. Yet of course, volunteering is ultimately good, even with all of these qualifications, because its existence recognizes that there are many who care deeply for others, who recognize the failure of social structures to provide what should be a basic right, and they work to address it to some degree.

More than ever, educational institutions recognize this important fact and find ways to encourage a community of giving and sharing. It is yet another way for us to create what Pope Francis has called a culture of encounter. For this to work, however, we must allow ourselves to be disempowered, overwhelmed and even at times humbled by the process of encounter. I once had a friend angrily complain that the homeless people he was reluctantly assisting didn't seem grateful enough for his help. When I asked if he was doing this for their gratitude, he seemed puzzled by the question. "No," he finally responded, "but it's the least they can do."

At a workshop held in a homeless shelter, one of our students asked a resident, "What's the most difficult part of being homeless?" I think we were all expecting a comment about the cold, the hunger or the loneliness. Instead, one man replied, "Being invisible. No one looks you in the eye." It was a humbling reminder that all of us, rich or poor, homeless or with homes, need the dignity of encounter, of human connectedness. It has become a cliché for people to remind us that the Holy Family were themselves homeless, and that their humble shelter was afforded to them only begrudgingly. But it is no less true. The Christmas miracle needs to be relived through story, but also through action. And we need to use this time to create a space for everyone to belong: even when it's uncomfortable to do so.

My Career as an Altar Boy

"At your service!"

2 Samuel 9:2

When I turned nine, I became an altar boy at the local church. I remember the lovely uniform I got to wear, and the exquisite smell of the incense in the change rooms. On my first day, the priest explained that I would lead the procession out into the church, carrying the gold crucifix on a long silver pole. "Hold it up proudly," he said, but he forgot to warn me about the low archway.

I was demoted to bell ringer. "Don't worry," he said, "I'll tell you when you're meant to ring them."

At the altar, during the most sacred ceremony on my first day of serving Mass, I looked out at the four people in the congregation. Two of these were my parents, who had fought their way through the worst snowstorm of the year to watch their son's great triumph. They were smiling up at me, waving surreptitiously. I was about to wave back when I felt the priest's foot poking me in the ribs. I looked up at him as he stood with the oversized host raised in his hands. He was looking up towards the ceiling, but his mouth was angled down.

"Now, boy. Ring the bell!" I started ringing for my life. The sound was magical. It reminded me of Christmas—of sleigh bells. I lowered my head and shut my eyes so tightly that I actually saw stars. And I rang those bells. I thought to myself, "No one will ever ring these as well or as loudly."

The priest kicked me sharply in the ribs and knocked the breath out of me. "For goodness' sake, knock it off!" he muttered. I stared up at him through watery eyes. "But you said…."

"Shh!" he whispered, slipping briefly into Latin, and then, correcting himself, repeating the words in English. He nudged me again, gently this time, and I let forth with another tremendous ring of the bells. He cut it short with such a sharp jab of his foot that I let out a yelp. Make up your mind, I thought angrily!

Later, because of my unfamiliarity with the vestments, I found that I was the last one in the change room. The priest seemed pleased to find me there. He moved in and poked his flushed face in my vicinity. He seemed terribly uncomfortable. I watched his mouth as he said, "Well, that wasn't so bad," and then only half understood as he explained that perhaps I wasn't cut out for this. Years later, when I thought about this time, I wondered insecurely if I was the only altar boy ever to be fired. At the time, though, I felt only relief.

Outside the church, in the blistering winter air, my mother hugged me tightly. She was crying. "You were *so* good," she said. "I'm sure you could hear those bells all over town."

Searching for Our Special Star

When they saw that the star had stopped,
they were overwhelmed with joy.

Matthew 2:10

This may seem like an odd question, but how many of you have ever wondered about Nativity scenes—in particular, when the first one (beside the obvious one in the Bethlehem stable) actually took place? Well, it never occurred to me to ask. My eyes were opened on this matter when I read an article about Pope Francis making a surprise visit to a Franciscan shrine in Greccio, Italy. There he knelt in front of a shrine created by his namesake. On Christmas Eve 1223, this was where St. Francis of Assisi purportedly erected the world's first Nativity scene.

Pope Francis would later tell a group of young people, on yet another impromptu visit, that this birth was an example of how "God lowered himself, obliterated himself to be like us, to walk before us, but with smallness, that is, you can say, humility, which goes against pride, self-importance, arrogance." And it was a star that led the Three Wise Men to this site, which prompted the Pope to insist that we look out for a "special star that calls us to do something greater, to strike out on a journey, to make a decision."

At St. Mary's University in Calgary, we organize under the banner of what we call the St. Mary's Star. Four qualities of Mary (simplicity, clarity, purity and confidence) are each represented

 by one of the four letter Ms that form the star. It is our commitment to students, and to the community, that we will honour all learners who come to our door, and because of our small class sizes that allow us to focus on the whole person, we truly believe that everyone has an opportunity to discover who they are. That is the remarkable gift of an education: that people can discover their own special star.

The truth about education is that while it is intensely personal, focused on self-improvement and intellectual development, it is also communal in so many ways, preparing students for their roles in the wider world. It is critical that all educational institutions support their students and encourage them to take their special talents out into the community. It is important for all learners to know that the gift they've received through their education is a shared gift—or perhaps is merely on loan. And for it to truly mature, it needs to be shared and turned towards a greater good. For that to happen, teachers must invite their students to search for their special star, knowing that together, in community, they will form or discover a dynamic constellation. And perhaps at Christmas this is one of the greatest gifts we can imagine.

The Empty Box

"You will find a child wrapped in bands of cloth."
Luke 2:12

There is a famous story of a struggling single father whose young daughter uses all of the expensive wrapping paper to cover a shoebox for her dad. On Christmas Day the impoverished father not only discovers this elaborately wrapped gift but finds, when he opens it, that the box is empty. Furious and thinking that his daughter is mocking him, he says angrily, "How could you waste all this paper, and why would you give someone an empty box as a present?" The child, upset, starts to cry. "But Daddy, the box isn't empty. I spent all day filling it with kisses just for you."

For me, the most remarkable and unexpected joy of being a father was in learning how to see the world through the eyes of my amazing children. It is not so much that you relearn what was difficult about childhood or teenage life. It is rather that you see the world through a different lens entirely. What may seem hugely important in an office conflict melts away into insignificance when a child teaches you kindness through the simplest acts. A store-bought gift can be made utterly inconsequential by a card that your child has spent half a day painting just for you.

The opening story, easily dismissed as overly sentimental, should remind us to look through new eyes at the gifts that come our way—gifts that may take many different forms and sizes. Education, for example, is not a neatly packaged product that you purchase and use like a hammer or a saw. It can be simply or elaborately packaged, but the gifts it offers can be unexpected, even hard to see in some respects, until the opportunity presents itself where these skills are called on and are made clear. Faith, too, appears invisible to many, and the gifts that Jesus offers can be readily missed or taken for granted. Sometimes it takes a shoebox moment to remind us that the box is full—the gift is infinite.

I can clearly identify the moments in my life, and in my education, where measurable skills were delivered and tasks taught. Similarly, I can call on my catechetical training to remember rituals and prayers. But what I learned through university and through my faith life is something else entirely. My belief in social justice, in my responsibility to my fellow citizen, in my responsibility to and for the other—this came not from direct study but from the example of faith and learning. From patient mentors, wise teachers, selfless priests and nuns, and good people everywhere.

When we open our gifts this Christmas, let us think of the empty boxes, filled with need, but replete, too, with goodness and hope. This, surely, is the true message of Christmas.

Also by Gerry Turcotte

The Oxford History of the Novel in Australia, Canada, New Zealand, and the South Pacific since 1950. Co-edited with Coral Ann Howells and Paul Sharrad. Oxford: Oxford University Press, 2017.

Small Things: Reflections on Faith and Hope. Toronto: Novalis, 2016.

Peripheral Fear: Transformations of the Gothic in Canadian and Australian Fiction. Brussels: P.I.E. Peter Lang, 2009.

Unsettled Remains: The Postcolonial Gothic in Canada. Co-edited with Cynthia Sugars. Waterloo, ON: Wilfrid Laurier Press, 2009.

Literary & Social Diasporas: An Italian Australian Perspective. Brussels: P.I.E. Peter Lang, Dec. 2007. Co-edited with Gaetano Rando.

Border Crossings: Words & Images. Australia: Brandl & Schlesinger, 2004.

hauntings: the 'Varuna' poems. Australia: Five Islands Press, 2003.

Winterlude. Australia: Brandl & Schlesinger, 2002.

Compr(om)ising Post/colonialism(s): Challenging Narratives and Practices. Co-edited with Greg Ratcliffe. Australia: Dangaroo, 2001.

Flying in Silence: A Novel. Canada: Cormorant Press/Hodder & Stoughton, 2001. Also published in Australia by Brandl & Schlesinger, 2001.

Canada–Australia: 1895–1995: Towards a Second Century of Partnership. Co-edited with Lois Foster and Kate Burridge. Ottawa: Carleton University Press, 1997.

Jack Davis: The Maker of History. Editor. Sydney: A&R/ HarperCollins, 1994.

Neighbourhood of Memory: Poems 1984–90. Denmark: Dangaroo Press, 1990.

Writers in Action: The Writer's Choice Evenings. Editor. Sydney: Currency Press, 1990.